SCATTERSHOT

My Journey from the Projects to Paris to Rodeo Drive

a memoir

LARRY CHRYSLER

*Helping talented writers
publish exceptional books.*

www.AcornPublishingLLC.com

For information, address:
Acorn Publishing, LLC
3943 Irvine Blvd. Ste. 218
Irvine, CA 92602

Scattershot
Copyright © 2024 Larry Chrysler

Cover design by Damonza
Interior design and formatting by Debra Cranfield Kennedy

Printed in the United States of America

ISBN-13: 979-8-88528-095-2 (hardcover)
ISBN-13: 979-8-88528-094-5 (paperback)
Library of Congress Control Number (LCCN): 2024903803

AUTHOR'S NOTE

I've always been recognized among my friends as someone who loves to talk. Whether it's over dinner or any casual setting, if a particular topic sparks a memory from my past, I dive into a narrative filled with intricate details. Admittedly, there have been occasions where I've been sometimes less than gently nudged to wrap up my story-telling, as I tend to extend the tales. Fortunately, I possess a vivid memory that allows me to effortlessly recollect events, people, and the emotions woven into those moments, so it wasn't long before the suggestion to document these stories in a book became a persistent refrain.

In 2007, I took the plunge into writing, penning down anecdotes about the myriad experiences and the fascinating individuals who colored my long and eventful life. Some of these encounters resulted in enduring friendships, while others remained fleeting acquaintances, leaving behind indelible imprints. As my words flowed onto the pages, I discovered moments that were humorous, titillating, and at times, deeply poignant. The process of crafting my first book became a cathartic journey, often accompanied by the shedding of a tear.

Within these pages, I share candidly the circumstances that shaped my world—moments that might evoke laughter, touch your heart, or even elicit a gasp of shock. This memoir is a collection of stories that reflect the tapestry of my life, a narrative that I hope inspires, resonates, and leaves you with an array of emotions.

DEDICATION

In fond memory of those dearly departed, who would probably be shaking their heads in disbelief that I, of all people, managed to string together more than two words and write this book.

CONTENTS

Touched By Angels

Do we realize life is predestined? Is it fate or kismet that guides us? I was sixteen when a stranger approached me on the street in downtown Minneapolis and told me she saw an angel on each of my shoulders. At the time, I thought she was some crazy lady and kept on walking. Yet ever since, I have navigated the turbulent rapids of life with something unknown guarding me.

I didn't know it at the time; in fact, I didn't take it seriously until after I moved to New York and then Los Angeles. Incredible opportunities and experiences kept happening regularly, and I understood that those angels weren't a fluke, that they were there to guide and protect me. The memory of that encounter has remained with me and given me a way to understand the unexpected and profound events in my life that otherwise have no sufficient explanation.

Long before I realized a career in fashion was to be my destiny, when I was five years old, my kindergarten class was given an assignment to construct a grocery store made of cardboard. Each student had to bring from home an empty, clean food container, make a new paper label for it, and add it to a display on the shelves of our "store." Once the shelves were fully stocked and our teacher, Miss Raleigh, had instructed us on the basics of operating a store, we took turns playing shopkeeper each day until everyone had gotten a chance to be in charge.

On the day I was to be the shopkeeper, a reporter and photographer from the *Minneapolis Star Tribune* were in our class to write a human-interest story about children learning the value of money at an early age. I posed behind the counter with my hair combed and neatly parted, smiling at the camera and pointing to my "wares" on the shelves. I loved getting all the attention I was getting and waiting on my fellow students; in fact, I may have loved it a bit too much.

The next day, when it was time for another student to be behind the counter, I refused to give up my position. I liked being there and I wasn't moving. Unable to reason with me, my teacher telephoned my mother and explained the problem. Exasperated, the teacher handed me the phone. Gently, Mother said I'd had my day and now it was another classmate's turn. I was to be a good boy and share it with the others.

I cried and reluctantly gave up my job, but it had already sparked the dream of owning a store, which I carried deep inside of me for years to come. Little did I realize at the time how the experience would foreshadow the life that lay before me.

To this day, I have never forgotten the glorious feeling of standing behind that counter. Even back then, I believe those angels the stranger had seen were by my side, leading me toward the person I was fated to be.

ONE

Who Is Rod Stewart?

It was April 1969 when I launched my first retail menswear store in Los Angeles. The shop was named after my friend and business partner at the time, Mike Bain, and the angels must have been watching over me, because our timing and location could not have been better.

The adjacent Sunset Strip was buzzing with hot shops and restaurants. Motown Records and Playboy opened offices directly across the street, giving us an instant and immediate fashion-conscious customer for our high-end, forward-thinking European clothing. In less than three months, the store became a popular hangout for customers—and celebrities—because of our casual and comfortable approach to fashion and shopping. They were just as eager to spend time in the store as they were to hang out at a trendy restaurant.

The first Christmas season was busier than we'd anticipated. Swamped by hordes of shoppers, we hired a young lady to wrap gifts on a card table set up in a corner of the store. The poor darling was so overwhelmed that when the legendary singer Diana Ross came in and saw her, she said, "Move over, honey, and let me help. I know how to wrap gifts." At the end of the day, Diana asked to use the telephone behind the cashier's desk and called her mother in Detroit.

"Mama," Diana said, "go next door and get Auntie. I am inviting both of you to my opening in Las Vegas."

That would be her first big Vegas concert. We knew better than to be starstruck, but even so, it never ceased to amaze me when celebrities visited our store and felt right at home.

The celebrity clientele loved coming by just to be there, to schmooze with their friends and know they wouldn't be bothered by the other equally affluent or famous customers. Popular Las Vegas stars Tom Jones and Engelbert Humperdinck often shopped together and teased one another about the way their new clothes fit.

Donald Sutherland was a size 42 long. He was going to be acting in a picture with Julie Christie in Italy and came in to ask me to design his wardrobe. Much of the film would be shot in Rome, and even though he would ultimately choose the Italian fabrics and sketch ideas I presented, the clothes would be made at Brioni Rome on the Via Condotti, where he could have his fittings done in person. His role was a schoolteacher whom I highly doubted could have afforded one piece of expensive Brioni clothing on a meager teacher's salary. I wasn't in the movie designer union, so I didn't get screen credit, but it was exciting working with Donald.

Our customer relationships often became personal, and Donald Sutherland was a warm and approachable person. I once checked into a small boutique hotel in London. When Donald signed in after me and saw my name in the guest book, he called my room and invited me to dinner. I had to decline the invitation because I had previous plans. Stupid me.

The inimitable Motown singer Isaac Hayes was another lovely customer. With his first royalty check in hand, he excitedly asked me to cash it instead of going to a bank the next morning. I happily obliged! How often can you say you got to cash the check of a man who made the movie *Shaft* a household name with its incredible soundtrack?

On any given Saturday, there were so many beautiful people shopping and engaging us in lively conversation that I would go home after work exhilarated and overly satiated by the experience.

On one such Saturday, John Lennon and Yoko Ono walked in wearing white T-shirts and faded blue jeans. I did my best to keep cool, introducing myself and offering our best salesman, Philippe Auber, to assist. After a few minutes, John came up and asked if I would mind if he didn't refold the sweaters after looking at them. Here was the great John Lennon asking me with the utmost sincerity when just the day before some mediocre TV actor had thrown merchandise all around after trying it on. Of course, we never heard of that TV actor after his one-season claim to fame.

John and Yoko had rented a house up the street behind the store and almost every day they came in to buy jeans and T-shirts. At the end of the summer, their houseman presented me with a signed photo of John, that said:

To Larry, With love and peace. John Lennon and Yoko Ono

1971. This photograph was autographed to me
by Lennon and Yoko Ono.
Copyright unknown. From the author's collection.

We did have our share of difficult customers and shoplifters just like any other store, but despite what most people would believe, the more important the star, the easier they were to interact with.

One Christmas, a well-known furniture store owner bought twenty-five gifts for each of her three sons. The day after Christmas I received an irate call from her. "You ruined Mikey's Christmas! He only received twenty-four gifts and his brothers got twenty-five!" Apparently, in the rush and craziness of the shopping season, our gift wrap person neglected to include the twenty-fifth gift. My apology fell on deaf ears until I finally blurted out, "Christmas? You're Jewish. What do you know about Christmas?"

Needless to say, I lost her as a customer, but her sons continued to shop with us.

Another time, Barbra Streisand's secretary called and asked if we would close the store for an afternoon so that Miss Streisand could shop discreetly. I explained nicely that we would be happy to have her come to the store, but we didn't close for anyone. Company policy. That was the only request of that type we ever had from a customer, and Barbra never ended up coming in.

Things tended to slow down in the summer, especially in the hot, smoggy middle of July when many folks were on vacation or lazing around by their pools. The store got particularly quiet during those periods, and I remember one day in particular which was no exception. The small parking lot in front was vacant and the store was empty of customers. A completely dead day. Suddenly, the front door opened, and in strode the one and only Elvis Presley, followed by four younger men. Elvis announced this was a new group he was promoting and would like them outfitted.

We showed the men velvet blazers and silk shirts, while Elvis wandered around the store pulling more clothing off the racks to be bought. During the tailor fittings, one of the men, in awe, confided to me that Elvis had just bought them a new Cadillac. While the group continued shopping, Elvis spotted a handmade silver and leather belt prominently displayed in a glass cabinet. He tried it on and then bought it for himself to wear at his upcoming Las Vegas opening. By the time Elvis left the building, the parking lot, which had been empty upon their arrival, was teeming with giddy, wide-eyed fans. He strode through that crowd like a pro who had done it all a thousand times before. Elvis was quiet, unassuming, and generous, and even without an audience his presence was unforgettable.

Not being very familiar with rock stars, I was sometimes unaware of their fame when they came into the store. One day, a man walked in carrying two shopping bags filled with very expensive boots he'd bought at a shoe store we'd opened a couple of doors down. He wandered around Mike Bain unassumingly choosing clothes he would casually hand to a salesman. When the salesman helped him approach the cashier with his arms laden with merchandise, I happened to be there to ring up the purchase. When I read the customer's name on his credit card, I discovered the man standing in front of me was Rod Stewart.

The name seemed vaguely familiar. I glanced up and said, "Oh, are you a painter?"

He smiled and said he did paint.

"Yes," I said, satisfied, "I knew I recognized your name."

The salesperson kicked me in the shin.

I had no idea who Rod Stewart was, but I certainly did after that day!

Buying clothing for retail is a guessing game. One never knows what's going to sell like crazy—or end up on the discount rack. There are winners and losers, and one fall season, I lost big.

Paris designers were showing knickers that year and for some reason I still have never quite figured out, I bought a huge number of them in corduroy. On the shelves for weeks, they didn't sell at all. Then hot pants became the fad of the next season, so, being resourceful, I had our tailor shop cut down the knickers to create short shorts. Those didn't sell, either. Still stuck with almost the original amount and not about to give up, I purchased leather straps. Then I had tailors cut and sew up the bottom of the hot pants and put the straps on them, thereby creating a corduroy shoulder bag. The third time was a charm. They sold like hotcakes.

On one of my Paris buying trips, the designer Jean-Paul Germain invited me to a dinner his mother Manouche was giving in his honor at the Left Bank eatery and nightclub Alcazar. Alcazar was bright and wonderfully stylish, with a fascinating history. Located right off the Boulevard St. Germain-Des-Près on a small but buzzing street and set on a seventeenth-century tennis court, Alcazar was once home to a notorious transvestite bar. The club next door was the infamous Rock 'n' Roll Circus, known as the last place Jim Morrison was seen partying before he passed away.

That evening, there were eight of us at the table. Sitting nearby at the banquette was the actress Melina Mercouri and her brother. Melina looked chic in a black dress, with her long blonde hair framing bright blue eyes. The broad smile on her face made a stark contrast to her brother's dour expression and Manouche's slightly red, boozy face and heavy red lips.

On stage, the host announced that Manouche was present, and the applause was deafening. Then he pointed out that the wonderful Melina Mercouri was in attendance as well, and the clapping was polite but not nearly as enthusiastic as it had been for Manouche. Upon hearing the applause for Mercouri, Manouche said very loudly in French, "At least I got a bigger hand than that bitch!" The comment was met with uproarious laughter and foot-stomping.

I was both amused and mortified and didn't know what to say to Jean-Paul. "Now you know what I go through with her," he said and downed the rest of his champagne.

Unlike buyers for large department stores, I was able to take time off to visit a museum and absorb the local sights during my twice-yearly buying trips to Europe. Le Club Sept was the trendiest bar-restaurant in Paris. On any given night there might be Paloma Picasso (the daughter of Pablo Picasso), the designers Yves Saint Laurent, Kenzo, Jean Paul Gaultier, and Karl Lagerfeld, or high-profile personages like Jackie Kennedy Onassis dining and dancing the night away. The place was always filled with celebrities until 4 a.m. The brasserie La Coupole was another hangout for models, designers, and buyers. We danced till the wee hours at Le Palace. Paris evenings during Fashion Week were always fun and intoxicating. There were times I almost forgot I was there to work not play.

Le Club Sept was where I met my first French boyfriend, Jackie LaFourcade. He was seated across the room on a banquette, and I couldn't stop staring at him. His eyes were as green as new grapes. When he caught me looking at him, he smiled shyly. The way he was dressed, in a crewneck Shetland sweater, corduroy pants, and loafers, he looked like he might have been American, but I was wrong. I went over to him and introduced myself, and he said he didn't speak English. After successfully trying to communicate in sign language (my French was rudimentary at best), I invited him to spend the night with me at the hotel Le Meurice where I was staying. At three in the morning, we entered the reception area only to be met by an imperious male receptionist demanding to know if "this gentleman" was a guest of the hotel. I said, "No, he is a guest of mine." And at that, we left the open-mouthed receptionist and were whisked upstairs in the elevator.

Jackie and I continued to see one another on my subsequent buying trips to France and my French improved enough so we could communicate verbally. (There is a saying that the best way to learn a foreign language is in bed.) He lived with his parents in Troyes, a small town in the Champagne country southeast of Paris, and I would stay the weekend there with him if I had enough time.

One weekend, we drove in his sleek, low-slung black Citroën from his home in Troyes to lunch in Dijon, where we spent a lovely afternoon. When it was time to return home, we glided along the deserted country roads as the sun disappeared behind heavy gray clouds and a light rain began to fall. The setting made me feel as though we were two characters in a François Truffaut film noir.

We were passing through the quaint village of Colombey-les-Deux-Églises when Jackie pointed to a large cemetery and said, "That is where 'Le General' is buried." I had just read that the famed General de Gaulle had recently died and was curious to see his tomb, so I suggested we go in.

We drove up to the high wrought-iron gates and were promptly stopped by a guard asking where we were going. He then informed us that the cemetery was closing shortly, at 5 p.m. Jackie pleadingly replied I was an American and had come all the way from California to see the grave of "Le General." Suddenly, the demeanor of the guard changed, and he saluted us, saying of course we could go in.

"It's an honor you've come so far, you're only the second American to visit the grave of Le General."

"Who was the first?" I asked.

Snapping to attention, he said, "President Nixon!"

For me, it was a dubious association to be sure, but a privilege nonetheless to visit the grave of General De Gaulle.

The Menswear Fashion Week in Paris was packed with buyers from around the world, and I was lucky enough to be one of thirty Americans among two hundred foreign buyers feted at a black-tie dinner dance each September hosted by the French Fashion Federation at a historical landmark site. The first I attended was at L'Orangerie in the Chateau Versailles. Not realizing the acoustics were sharp, I walked in with a buyer friend from the I. Magnin San Francisco store and, standing in the entrance, said in what I thought was almost a whisper, "We made the palace, baby." Above the din, my voice unmistakably carried through the room, and I was instantly embarrassed. It seemed like every guest looked over at me—some laughing, others scowling.

Another year, dressed in my Armani tuxedo and carrying a martini in my hand, I tripped and fell on one of the fragments of Roman pillars strewn about the garden of a twelfth-century church. Still holding the martini glass and not having spilled a drop, I looked up at the group I was with and said, "I know how to fall. I used to be an ice skater!" Of course, I'd ripped a hole in the leg of my tux, but I think I managed to pull off the rest of the evening without anyone noticing but me.

Those European buying trips were not all fun and games. I usually got off the plane at 7 a.m. after a ten-hour flight and had to be at my first appointment just a few hours later, then work without a break until dinner. Many times, international buyers suffering from jet lag would take a quick nap in their respective hotels before going out to dinner, only to wake up late or sleep through the night. It happened to me multiple times.

Pitti Uomo in Florence, Italy was another major destination where I would travel twice a year. The Italians sold beautiful, expensive clothing, and it was a city where I always worked late and didn't have much time for amusement other than dinners before heading off to bed.

On one of those trips, I had been at an appointment later than I thought, so I rushed out, grabbed a taxi, and urged the driver to speed to the small airport so I'd be on time to catch my plane to London. Frantic that I'd miss my flight, I jumped out of the taxi when we arrived at the airport and ran inside, where people were still waiting to board the plane. Happy and relieved I'd made it on time, I checked my suitcase and quickly went into the men's room. While standing at the urinal, I noticed a handsome man lingering and staring at me. When I finished urinating, he motioned for me to follow him into a stall. It was such a different time back then, sometimes you had to seize an opportunity when it presented itself. Nervous yet aroused, I looked at my watch and figured I had just enough time.

In the stall, as he proceeded to fellate me, I repeatedly looked at my watch, and each time I did he would look up, shake his head no, and continue. After my orgasm, I rushed out just as the passengers were about to board. As we approached the plane, the captain and crew were there to greet us. Sure enough, the man I'd met was the captain. Of course, we had time in the stall: we weren't going anywhere until he was on board! When I approached the crew, he shot me a knowing smile and said, "*Buon Giorno.*"

Ah, Italia!

TWO

Sartorial Bloodlines

My mother's family came from Latvia. In the capital of Riga, my grandmother had been a hat designer, while my grandfather worked in a clothing store. Around 1910, when my mother's siblings and parents arrived in St. Paul, my grandfather began selling clothing from his horse and wagon, traveling all over Minnesota to meet with the Chippewa Indians and farmers eager to buy his wares.

Shortly after the kindergarten episode, Mother told him the story of how much I'd loved being a shopkeeper. My grandfather suggested I accompany him to what he referred to as "the wholesale house." That way I could see where and how he chose the clothing he was going to sell.

I was thrilled with the idea and couldn't wait to go. At last, the big day arrived. Grandpa (looking natty in a tightly buttoned, dark gray worsted wool suit) and I (dressed in my best sweater and knickers) took a long streetcar ride to a large warehouse at the end of the line, where we stood gazing at the drab building. "This is it!" Grandpa exclaimed. "The wholesale house!" Then he took my hand and walked me proudly to the front door.

Upon entering, we were warmly greeted by the salespeople, who led us into a cavernous room with wall-to-wall shelves filled with men's clothing neatly piled in labeled categories.

"Now watch this," he said, as he began to pull shirts, pants, and wool jackets from the shelves. "These will be perfect for my customers up north. They are going to love all this stuff."

He seemed to have each one of his customers in his mind as he searched the shelves, as if knowing exactly what they would want to buy. I was fascinated watching the selection process and seeing the clothing being thrown into boxes. I think he noticed how exciting it was for me to be there. At one point, he leaned down and said into my ear, "Now it's your turn. Go on and pick a few things out you'd like me to try and sell."

His big hands lifted me to the shelves, and I grabbed some shirts, giddily throwing them into an open box.

"Now we count the merchandise," he said.

After carefully counting, each piece was written on an order pad he'd carried in with him. Then one of the salesmen recounted and invoiced everything. Grandpa himself sealed the boxes, explaining to me in a whisper, "These people are not to be trusted, and there might be missing a piece or two when the boxes are delivered and loaded on my wagon."

Five years old and that single afternoon taught me almost all I would need to know to start my own clothing business decades later: how to prepare the shelves, how to think about the customers, how to treat the vendors, how to keep an eye on everything and everyone so that you don't lose any product or money.

And, most importantly, how to do what you love.

Fast forward to when destiny rang again. A similar scenario

happened in Paris. The year was 1969, I was thirty-eight years old and buying for the grand opening of our retail store Mike Bain. I'd read in *Women's Wear Daily* that dress designer Jean Cacharel had created his first collection of men's jersey shirts, and they were a sensation. When I called his office for an appointment, I was told I had to go directly to their warehouse on the outskirts of Paris to choose the shirts because the inventory was sparse. Also, I'd heard from another buyer it was safer to have the salesman seal the boxes in front of me because they were known for slipping out a few items before shipping. As I stood there watching the shirts being carefully counted and invoiced, I suddenly had a sense of déjà vu—it was just like Grandpa had taught me all those years ago in St. Paul.

I was born on August 16, 1931, in Minneapolis, Minnesota. My parents had been married only one month when Mother became pregnant with me. I'm told Dad said it was too soon to have a baby because he had no money to support a family, but abortion was unheard of, at least publicly, and after nine months, there I was out in the world.

My first "outing," but not my last.

My name, Lawrence, was given to me in honor of the man who delivered produce by horse and wagon in our neighborhood. Because my parents were poor, he kindly gave them free fruit and vegetables for many years. My middle name, Bernard, in the Jewish tradition of naming a newborn after a deceased relative, respected the memory of a great-uncle who, as family stories went, was single, handsome, and traveled the world, always bringing beautiful gifts home for his sisters. "And he never married," was the tagline that always followed, which, of course, I'd later find out was often code for being gay, though nobody in our family ever confirmed it one way or the other.

My two namesakes foretold certain qualities that I have tried to emulate throughout my life: kindness, generosity, and worldliness. Although in the Jewish religion, a child is not named after a living relative, I would have taken my father's name, had it been possible, because he exposed me to so many of the cultural passions that would ultimately enrich my life in myriad ways. Also, it might have been Max Winters, a kindly friend of the family (who was the father of the first manager of the Minneapolis Lakers basketball team), because it was old Mr. Winters who bought me a tricycle and an entire cowboy outfit, including fur chaps, holster, and pistols. I rode that tricycle like a horse 'round and 'round a small park across the street from my grandmother's house dreaming I was riding the range. I would have loved being named Max, in honor of a man known for his love and generosity.

My father, Jack, was born in Boston. A trained operatic baritone with a thrilling voice, he suffered from severe sinus infections that plagued him throughout his life and sidelined him from having an opera career. He played the violin and saxophone, spoke five languages fluently, and studied dentistry at the University of Minnesota, dropping out after only one year.

Even as a child, it was the anticipation of hearing Dad's wonderful voice singing opera arias in the car on the long way home from a boring day of fishing that made the day worthwhile. A disinterested kid like me had to sit on a pier in the hot sun, put a worm on a hook, and then wait to catch a fish. After catching the damned thing, having to take it off the hook was too much, and I would complain the rest of the day. Dad would be angry about my squeamishness and would call me a "fraidy cat" and "sissy," but once we were in the car he would forget about his anger and begin to sing my favorite aria, *Vesti la giubba* from Leoncavallo's opera *Pagliacci*. Hearing him sing the character of the clown's sob at the end of it always brought tears to my eyes. It was then and only then that he'd put his arm around me before singing more arias, which always included the Italian folk song *La Signora* and its opening lyrics, *Di spagna sono la bella* ...

During the early Depression, Dad worked hard loading trucks for a great uncle's company, Brooks Produce, for seven dollars a week. There was no market for any of his musical talents and that job was given to him only because he was a relative and it was the only work available to him during those difficult financial years.

Just for fun and using his musical talent, Dad put together a small dance band. On weekend nights, he began playing at local clubs, bar mitzvahs, and weddings. But even with the supplementary income from those jobs, he still wasn't making enough to buy the necessary sheet music for the band.

My mother, however, had a perfect ear and tonal memory. She listened to all the latest songs on the radio, which she'd then sing or whistle back to my father, enabling him to transcribe onto paper the musical arrangements for each of the band members.

Dad would regularly scour the ads in the newspaper looking for a different line of work than loading trucks. One time, he saw an opening for a band to play a two-week gig at a nearby summer resort. The resort was known for prohibiting Jewish membership and with our very Jewish family name of Cohen, getting the job would be out of the question. But the opportunity and money were too great for Dad to ignore. He applied for the gig anyway, putting his pride aside and changing his last name to Collins. The band was not only hired but Dad, being the band leader, was allowed to bring along his wife and me, his son. However, that presented one small problem. I had to remember my new name. In the weeks leading up to our leaving, Mom made it her job to insist I start using our new last name, repeatedly drilling me, a five-year-old, to remember the name, Collins.

When we arrived at the resort, Mother, and I in my favorite yellow linen sunsuit, had some time to kill before dinner and the evening entertainment, so we walked down a path to the beach. A woman approached us and commented to Mother that I was a darling child. Then, she turned to me.

"And what is your name, little boy?" she asked.

I could feel Mother freeze and hold her breath.

I looked up and smiled confidently. "Larry Collins," I said, and Mother exhaled.

That was the first time I learned to fake it. There would be other times during my life when I would fake things, but I suppose what I learned then was that at certain times faking it was all it took to give me the nerve and strength to get through a particular situation.

My mother, Mary, led a simple life as a devoted housewife. She had never learned to cook, but she put a lot of effort into preparing good meals and maintaining a clean home for us. Her cheerful demeanor was infectious, and she would frequently wander around the house, humming and singing to herself. There were moments when she'd look at us amazed and say, "I have no idea how I raised you children," a statement I believe also alluded to the challenges posed by her physical and mental health issues.

Muscular dystrophy developed when she was in her twenties and continued to weaken her legs throughout her life, often causing her to unexpectedly fall. It got so bad over the years that at one point, around 1944, pregnant and walking in the living room, her legs suddenly gave out and she collapsed, resulting in a miscarriage. I was twelve at the time and cried at seeing my mother so vulnerable.

Later, when I was in my thirties, she fell and broke both kneecaps. It was hard to watch her deteriorate and struggle both physically and emotionally, but, even so, she was determined to keep on walking. Finally, when it became necessary to use a cane, she felt embarrassed, saying to me, "Oh Larry, look at how weak I've become, having to use a cane."

I remember hugging her and trying to lift her spirits, saying, "Mom, you look very chic walking with a cane."

After a while, however, it became more and more obvious that despite getting over the shame she once had about walking, the disease was increasingly debilitating, forcing her to walk slowly and making huge demands on her body. Waiting to cross a particularly busy street one day in downtown Minneapolis, with her new cane in hand, she made her way slowly into the crosswalk after the light turned green. An impatient driver honked at her and yelled something out the window, and that was all it took for Mom to pivot towards the car and smash its right headlight with the end of her cane.

After the police brought her home and she told me the story, I realized how terrible she felt about the incident, but I wanted to continue giving her the courage to keep on walking, so I told her I thought she'd done the right thing.

"You should have smashed them both, Mom," I said, and she laughed.

Over time, despite relying on a cane, her legs continued to falter during short to moderate walks. Years later when they moved to California, Dad began taking her to Palisade Park in Santa Monica and supporting her as they strolled together along the pathways.

I am my mother's son. We have the same big blue eyes, and from her I inherited my determination and optimism. The idea of persisting regardless of the circumstances was a trait she embodied, often summed up with the phrase, "Keep on trucking along," as we used to say.

My sister Sandra was born when I was almost four years old. I saw her for the first time in my mother's arms when they came home from the hospital. She lay there crying with a mouth open as big as her little head. All through her childhood, Dad called her the Yiddish word "pisher." *Pisher* is a person who pees a lot but is also slang for a crybaby, and the word applied to her. When we were children and my parents were away from the house on Saturday shopping forays, Sandy would pick fights with me. She'd jump on my back and pound away with her little fists and I would be laughing because she was so tiny, it didn't hurt. Then, the moment my dad came home, she would start bawling, claiming I had hit her.

"I'll teach you to hit a little girl," Dad would say, then he'd haul off and slap me.

Yes, that was my dad and my sister, Sandy. Yet with all her crying and conniving, I still adored her. Dad may have called her pisher, but because she was so little and cute, I nicknamed her "Peanut."

1937. Sandy and I were two Depression kids.
From the author's collection.

Until I was eight, we lived on Humboldt Avenue North in a lower middle-class neighborhood on the north side of Minneapolis. Our second-floor duplex apartment was near Sumner Field, a large park where I learned to ice skate at the age of three. I loved to skate and learned on single-blade skates. When Dad was a teenager he'd played hockey, and by the time my feet reached the size of his old hockey skates, he gave them to me.

Every winter, I would go to the park to skate or slide down the small hills on a large piece of cardboard. My parents couldn't afford to buy me a sled, that's how poor we were.

Often, some of the other boys with sleds would try to run me off the hill, but once I caught on, I would purposely push my cardboard in front of them. That usually resulted in snowball fights and tumbling in the snow.

I realized I was less advantaged than some of the other kids, but as a child, I had no idea how poor we were. My corduroy knickers were threadbare at the knees and my well-worn stockings were always falling, but I learned through the rest of my life to pull those metaphorical stockings up and start all over again.

We lived just a few miles from Lake Calhoun. When I was four years old, Dad took me there to teach me to swim. Before putting me in the water, he carried me in his arms, wading out until the water was up to his chest. Then, he began to throw me in the air, pretending not to catch me. I remember screaming and crying, thinking he was about to drop me in the deep water.

Angry with me for acting like such a baby, he left me with a stranger on the beach while he went for a swim. The terror of that experience caused a fear of drowning that lasted until my adulthood, and it taught me not to trust him at a very young age, all but killing any sense of comfort I had.

I have been told that at five years old I was not only curious about everything but also feisty and independent. Once, angry with my parents about something or other, I stuffed clothes in a paper bag and threatened to go live with our next-door neighbors, the Treat family. They were a Black family with two boys: Coby, my best friend, and his older brother, Teddy. I spent many happy days playing at their house, but I never did make good on my threat to move in with them. Years later, when I went to see the movie *The Jerk*, starring Steve Martin, and saw the opening scene of him trying to awkwardly dance on a porch with the Black family he lived with, I thought, "Oh my God, that could have been me had I gone to live with Coby and his family."

On nearby Lyndale Avenue, there was a storefront Holy Roller church that Coby and I often walked to. We would stand in front of the screen door listening to the gospel music and the shouts of the congregation praying. The sound of the emotional singing was thrilling to us, and we tried to join in by yelling out joyful boyish screams. There was something about the sound of that singing that electrified me, and to this day the sound of gospel singing brings back those memories.

When I was six, Mother thought Dad and I might bond better if the two of us spent some father-son time alone together. The Ringling Brothers circus had come to town, and she suggested he take me to see it. Despite our differences, we were both excited at the idea, and I remember feeling like I was about to see something no one else had ever seen before, some secret universe only known to grownups and adventurous spirits. At the circus, we sat in the cheapest seats, way off to the side, and for a small kid like me, it was difficult to see any of the main action. My neck was sore from trying to watch the acrobats and clowns farther down the arena, so I concentrated on the maintenance crew cleaning up the elephant dung directly in front of us instead. Dad, oblivious to my discomfort, was surprised when we came home, and I excitedly told my mother how big the dung was and nothing else about the circus. He still could not understand me even though he thought he'd made the effort.

There were times when Dad was caring—or tried to be—but I continued to be wary, walking on eggshells whenever I was around him. One of the ways he attempted to show compassion was on my birthday, when he would bake and decorate a cake and help me blow up balloons to decorate the house for my parties. As soon as my friends arrived, he turned into Mr. Charming, reveling in their compliments about the cake, balloons, and decorations, while I, the birthday boy, was ignored and shunted somewhere off to the side. Because of this, I grew up dreading my birthdays, knowing what was going to happen each time. When I was older and made enough money to finally be able to buy him a gift for his birthdays, inevitably he would disparage the item, saying how poorly it was made. I never could win with him.

Until the day he died, Dad and I had a dreadful time understanding and getting along with one another. I grew to be fearful of him until I became an adult, but as a child, I was always on guard for his getting angry with me about one thing or another. His sister Sally would ask, "Jack, why do you make Larry cry?" Mother often asked the same question.

It wasn't until I was in my forties when my mother's psychiatrist at UCLA asked my sister Sandy and me to come in for a meeting during one of her stays at the neuropsychiatric hospital. Before he mentioned our mother, he said, "Are you aware your father is a latent homosexual?"

Sandy and I looked at one another and nodded. Neither of us was surprised by his diagnosis. Sandy and I had always felt that the ongoing difficulties between Dad and me were because he saw me in himself. He spoke so often of how he enjoyed wrestling with his uncle Teddy when they were both in college together that it reached a point where we would cringe whenever we heard the oft-repeated story. Our ongoing feeling was that he had admired and still loved that uncle. Although latent homosexuality helped to validate the doctor's diagnosis and helped us to contextualize certain of our father's behaviors, we felt certain Dad had never acted on any of his homosexual feelings.

One day I overheard Dad explaining to my mother's brother his feeling that I would grow up to be a "fairy." My uncle said he knew how to make a man out of me and offered to send me to the prestigious Blake Academy, an elite military school where they would take care of the "problem." When the proposal was raised to send me away, I put up such a fuss that my mother intervened and convinced my dad not to do it. As usual, she was always mediating in our house, trying to "make nice" whenever one of the many disputes arose between my father and me—and this was a big one. To this day, though, I regret not attending the Academy, because in later years I was told by an alumnus that sex between the students was commonplace. My big mistake. I'd have to wait!

I adored my Uncle Irving and always thought of him as Cary Grant: sophisticated and handsome with big brown eyes and long lashes, dressed beautifully, drove a convertible, played golf, and had lots of girlfriends. He lived at home with his parents until he married at age forty.

Every Sunday, Sandy and I were taken by my parents to visit my grandparents' house. On the streetcar going to St. Paul, I would inevitably throw up from motion sickness. Then, once we arrived, I would wait for the first opportunity to sneak into my uncle's bedroom and open his dresser drawers so I could admire his cufflinks, ties, and neatly folded shirts, basking in the scent of his cologne still permeating the room. One Sunday, when he said he was going to take a nap, I innocently asked if I could nap with him, but he replied with an adamant "No!"

I believe he was much more worldly and comfortable with himself than my dad, and that he had me all figured out.

Uncle Irving wasn't going to give up on me, though, and thinking it would do me good he took me to his lakeside club, the Calhoun

Beach Club. As we walked to the locker room, we passed a dozen or so naked men lying in the sun on a terrace. Fascinated by their exposed genitals, I tried not to look but couldn't help myself. My homosexuality was lurking within me, just waiting to burst.

What I realize now, even if I couldn't see it for a good many years, is that in their different ways, my uncle and father were trying their best to look out for me. At times, it might have come out sideways and angrily from my father, or a place of complete repression, but in so many other ways my uncle and my father also expanded my notion of the world and taught me how to enjoy the finer things in life: the arts, classical music, fashion, and more.

I'd always been a somewhat devious and yet vulnerable kid, despite my independence. One autumn when I was eight years old, I stole a dollar out of my mother's purse so that I could go to the local grocery store to buy candy. After I bought the candy bar, I asked the clerk to give me the change in dimes. As soon as I arrived home, I proceeded to put the dimes in a hole I'd dug next to a backyard tree so that I could keep them safe and use them some other day.

Unbeknownst to me, I had been observed digging the hole by the workman hired by our landlord. He was a man in his early twenties, one of the many men known as "drifters," who roamed the country looking for work during the Great Depression.

The following day he came to me in the garden and told me he'd seen me hide the money but would not tell my parents nor would he take the money if I came into the shed with him. I naively agreed and followed him into the darkened shed. Once we were inside, he immediately closed the door, pulled me close to him, and took out his penis. He then put my hand in his hand and had me masturbate him.

Even though I had seen an adult male's penis before, this time I knew something bad was happening and I got scared, but as fearful as I was about what might happen to me, it was mixed with the slightest tinge of excitement as well.

Afterward, he hugged me and said, "This is our secret, so now we both have a secret to keep."

I readily agreed and promised to keep it a secret.

When he opened the door and we walked out into the bright sunshine, I skipped off feeling as though it had been a dream, and quickly put the incident out of my mind.

The next day, I took some of the dimes to school and gave them to my friends who, in turn, told their parents how they'd gotten the money. At school the next morning, I was called into the principal's office where my mother sat looking very angry and teary-eyed. The principal said she knew of my "crime" and then she whacked me across my knuckles with a ruler, sending me home with my mother. That night when Dad came home, he was as furious as ever and gave me a good spanking. I never stole again.

<hr />

On December 7, 1941, my friends and I were building a snowman in the front courtyard of our apartment building. Suddenly, windows opened wide, and we heard radios blaring the news that the Japanese had attacked Pearl Harbor. I was ten years old.

Immediately, America mobilized, and citizens were asked to donate anything made of metal to what was called the Scrap Drive. Dad, being a patriotic American, decided to donate all the pewter candlesticks that had been in his mother's family in Boston. He handed Sandy and me a hammer and said, "Go to it, kids." Mother wept.

Times had always been tough for us, but they got tougher for everyone during the war. Air raid drills and rations became a way of life, and we sat by the radio nightly listening to reports on the fighting overseas. But even in the darkest days, we found ways of keeping hope alive for better days ahead, even if we couldn't imagine what they'd look like.

On Thanksgiving the following year, Dad was very ill with pneumonia. If there was one characteristic of Dad's that delighted me the most, it was his sense of humor no matter how dire the situation. Despite being broke and sick as a dog, he was determined to celebrate the holiday. When we sat down at the dining room table, we were met not with baskets of warm rolls and boats full of piping hot gravy and a carved turkey, but with empty plates upon which my father had placed handwritten notes labeled "turkey," "cranberry sauce," and "mashed potatoes." Our actual meal was to be very inexpensive salami, sardines, and bread, but Dad wanted us to have the sense that we could enjoy the traditional Thanksgiving meal if we just put a little bit of imagination into it.

But what was in store for us that Thanksgiving turned out to be much more than Dad's food labels. Just as we sat down, there was a knock on the door. When I ran to open it, there stood two uniformed Salvation Army men holding bags of kosher Thanksgiving food for us. Mother cried seeing them and I couldn't stop hugging my sister. I still don't know if Dad knew they were showing up that day, but I suspect he didn't because even he looked surprised once he understood what was going on. I never forgot that moment in time, and ever since then, the importance of charity has remained inside of me.

As soon as I had the means, I started donating to others who were less fortunate to help them celebrate Thanksgiving just as our family had. Not only that, but that day also taught me the power of imagination and belief. My father believed in giving us a better Thanksgiving, even if it meant putting out little labels, and I've often wondered if our believing in those labeled dishes is what made the reality and miraculous gift come through that day.

Just before the war, Dad got a good job working as a draftsman for the City Planning Commission, where he joined a team creating the Sumner Field Housing Project. After months of long hours and hard work, he came home one day to excitedly announce that the public housing development had been completed—and we were going to be the first family to move in. First Family! The sound of that was wonderful, and it felt like the tide had finally started to turn in our favor financially.

The Sumner Field Projects covered four blocks of a racially divided (Black and White) community consisting of two three-story buildings and a few blocks of two-story buildings. We moved into the top floor of one of the three-story buildings. I'll never forget the feeling of walking into a brand-new apartment, where nothing, not even the toilet, had ever been used. It was as if it had been made especially for us.

The projects were across the street from Sumner Field Park, which had a pond that served as an ice rink in the winter where I would skate until I was called into dinner. I loved racing and playing hockey the most, and I can't even imagine how many total hours I spent out there gliding across the ice.

The neighborhood we lived in was a racial, ethnic, and religious mixture of poor people. It was the projects, after all. Although we were the only Jews in the housing development, I don't remember hearing any anti-Semitic sentiments. However, when I was about eleven, some of the local boys said they wanted to go a few streets away to beat up what they called the "sheenys" (a derogatory term for Jews). At that, one of them looked at me and said, "But not you, Larry. You're different."

Something else rang a bell in me when they said the word "different"—something that felt like a secret they'd found out about. It wasn't only the fact that I was Jewish, but something else that I didn't quite yet understand.

The boys they wanted to fight with lived in a more upscale neighborhood and my friends considered them "rich Jews," making them a target for us kids in the projects. I lived in the projects though, and therefore I was one of them, making me, in their estimation, "different" than those other Jewish boys.

I'd come to find out what that *other* difference was soon enough before long, the neighborhood boys and I did fight, but not because of any differing religious ideologies. No, they came after me because I didn't give in or respond to their increasingly frequent taunts on the way to and from school. Whenever they'd yell "Larry the fairy!" I'd pretend not to hear them, and repeat the old truism to myself, "Sticks and stones may break my bones, but names will never hurt me." I would keep on walking, holding my head up high, and that aloof attitude of mine would invariably annoy them to the point that they would chase me down and pummel me. If my tiny sister Sandy ever saw this fracas, she would run into the apartment yelling, "Where's the baseball bat? Gimme the bat. They're beating up on Larry!" Or she would join in the fight straight away, jumping on one of the boys and pounding her little fists until they started laughing. These encounters always left me slightly disheveled but never resulted in any serious physical injuries or tears. Even so, it was these early instances of being picked on, both by my father at home and by the boys in the neighborhood, that made me throw myself all the harder into the things I did love and that I could maintain control over.

When we eventually moved to one of the two-story buildings, I told Dad I wanted to study the piano. The previous year Dad had encouraged me to study the saxophone, but I'd grown tired of dragging it to Grant Grade School, and I'd always been enamored by the sound of the piano. Dad reluctantly agreed despite not even owning a piano. So, I began taking lessons at the Phyllis Wheatley Settlement House just a few blocks away. It cost twenty-five cents an hour to study the John Thompson Piano Method with the teacher Miss Roach.

Because we didn't have a piano at home for me to practice on, Dad told me a story of a famous German-Jewish concert pianist who had been incarcerated in a concentration camp in Germany just before the Second World War. To continue playing the music in his mind, he made a keyboard out of cardboard, and imagining the sound helped him to endure the hardship of the camp until his rescue. That seemed perfectly logical to me, so Dad tore apart a big old box and made me the same kind of keyboard. For the next week, I sat at the dining room table painstakingly clumping away at my cardboard keyboard, never the wiser. And then my piano life changed.

On the following Saturday, upon returning home from my lesson, I walked into the apartment, and there in the living room was an upright Kimball piano. I could hardly believe my eyes. I was so excited I ran outdoors yelling and doing summersaults all over the lawn.

Even though we lived in the projects, our quality of life had improved significantly to the point where Dad was able to surprise me by buying a piano. From then on, I would fight my sister for practice time until she gave up taking lessons altogether. The importance of having that piano enabled me to understand and deepen my love for music. In so many ways, that piano saved my life. I clung to it with everything I had from the moment I first laid my eyes on it.

When school began in the fall, by moving a couple of blocks away from our other apartment we had crossed the invisible border between my racially mixed grade school and a Black school. It was frightening being the only white kid and needing to have my friends Coby and Teddy, who'd lived next door to me on Humboldt Avenue, walk me home after school and protect me against the bullies, who were meaner than the ones who used to call me Larry the fairy. In particular, there was a tough little Black girl I called "The Girl With No Teeth in Front," who was so young her adult teeth still hadn't grown in yet. None of us knew her real name, but she was a real little toughie, always fighting with the boys.

Finally, the next semester, my mother lied to the school authorities about another change of address, and I was moved back to Grant, my former grade school.

As encouraging as my parents were about following my musical passion, they also knew, because of my father's unsuccessful attempts to become a professional opera singer, that I would need to learn a good work ethic regardless of what my future professional life entailed. I started working when I turned eleven, and my first job was delivering morning newspapers to the nearby African American community. At five o'clock in the morning, I would go to the local distribution center, take my allotted newspapers, fold them carefully, and put them in a bag mounted on my bike. Then, upon arriving at the designated address, I tossed the papers in front of the house or apartment doors. Inevitably, at that hour, there would be dogs copulating in the street and I was fascinated watching them, learning about sex. Now and then a house door would open, and a man would come out with a plastic cap presumably covering hair-straightening cream on his head.

I enjoyed riding my bike through the city before everybody was awake, but even more than that, I enjoyed watching my jar of money fill up at home. After six months, with the money I saved from that job, I was able to buy my first piece of clothing: a chartreuse long-hair Angora vest. In retrospect, I am sure it was awful looking, but I loved it, and I loved the freedom of having selected it myself. From that day forward, I never again had my parents choose my clothes.

THREE

Changes

In my teen years, my love of the arts, particularly music and fashion, took off, launching me on a trajectory that would span the next five decades. This was partly due to some great teachers I had, my stubborn insistence that I pursue what made me truly happy, and, last but not least, my old friend fate, which provided me with multiple serendipitous opportunities that radically changed my life.

I continued studying the piano until I was thirteen when Miss Roach suggested my musical education would be better served if I changed teachers because I was proceeding rapidly and able to play more difficult pieces. She recommended an esteemed teacher named Elsie de Wolfe Campbell, a tall, voluptuous woman in her forties who always wore ruffled floral dresses. Soon thereafter, I began taking Saturday lessons with her at the MacPhail Center for Music.

Pianists know that the foundation of a good education is learning the music of the composer Bach, but for whatever reason, other than playing only one piece by the composer, I was never given another. I did, however, learn plenty of Beethoven, Debussy, Chopin, and

Mozart, among others, as well as two-piano music, which I played with a couple of her other students or with Miss Campbell herself.

There were two side-by-side baby grand pianos in her studio and one summer she suggested we play something just for fun—a summer diversion. I happily learned the Count Basie book of *Boogie Woogie* and we banged away together on those two pianos, my summer-tanned fingers flying over the keys.

Usually after my Saturday morning piano lesson, Sandy and I would go to White Tower and buy two greasy hamburgers loaded with grilled onions for fifteen cents. We'd take them to the State movie theater and sit up on the balcony where we'd eat them, the pungent smell of onions wafting over the audience below.

I was an ardent piano student, practicing an hour in the morning and two after school. I dreamed of becoming a concert pianist. My bedroom walls were covered with RCA Victor record company posters of famous musicians, such as the opera singer Lily Pons, pianist Arthur Rubinstein, and conductor Leopold Stokowski. I figured I would educate our nearby neighbors by putting my phonograph against the open window and blasting out classical music in the early evenings, and I grew my hair long so I looked more like a serious musician. If I ever stayed home from school with an illness, I would find my way to the piano, get lost in my music, and immediately recover. At a time when I was convinced the world misunderstood me and that I was born in the wrong time and place, or at least to the wrong family, the piano was my salvation.

At thirteen years old, puberty was kicking in, and fuzz started growing on my face. Dad told me not to shave because once I started, there was no turning back.

I prepared for my Bar Mitzvah, hating every minute of learning Hebrew from a great uncle-rabbi who equally detested me. The plaid suit I chose to wear at the synagogue ceremony was like one I'd seen in a photo of the stylish Prince of Wales. On my Bar Mitzvah day, I sang my lessons for the Saturday congregation, and according to Jewish tradition, I became a man, though I didn't feel much different than I had the day before.

On the first day of eighth grade at Lincoln Junior High, I was still wearing knickers as I always had till then, but when I saw how the other boys were dressed, I realized I was sartorially way out of step. As soon as I got home after school, I demanded my parents buy me long pants like the other boys were wearing. Also, since I was now a freshman in junior high school, I let it be known that I no longer wanted to speak to Sandy because, after all, she was just a child. Puberty was doing strange things to not only my body but also my mind.

Then love struck. Her name was Barbara Brown. I'd met her at an inter-school dance where we danced cheek to cheek to the song "Time After Time." Barbara lived in a large house on the more affluent side of town close to the shore of Lake Calhoun. Her parents were not too happy about Barbara and me wanting to spend time together. I was a kid from the wrong side of the tracks, and they envisioned someone different for their daughter, though we were only thirteen. In the end, the logistics of going to different schools and living so far apart ended our brief romance. There were other girls at school I danced with, but not until high school was I smitten again.

Meanwhile, my sexual exploration with boys continued. How could I like girls and also be fooling around with boys? All I knew was that I enjoyed both, and I decided that girls were for love and that boys were for sex. *C'est tout*! That question about myself, like so many other questions, passed from my thoughts and my life blithely went on.

I had enjoyed having my own money after my summer job delivering newspapers, and wanted to find another part-time job so that I could buy better clothes for myself and go out more often. The Help Wanted pages in the newspaper advertised an opening for a Page at the Radisson Hotel, so I wrote down the address and immediately took a bus there. The original privately-owned Radisson Hotel and the Curtis Hotel were two of the most expensive in town. I looked older than my thirteen years, so I applied for the job saying I was sixteen and could work Monday evenings and weekends. I was promptly hired.

Hotel Pages wore red uniforms with small red or black pillbox hats perched at an angle, and they were responsible for calling out the name of a hotel guest either in the lobby or the bar to inform them of a telephone call or message left at the reception desk. I loved roaming the hotel's public rooms to announce in my cracking, pubescent voice, "Calling Mr./Mrs. So-and-So!"

The one place I hated going into was the Viking Room bar. It was always jam-packed with soldiers and sailors drinking, smoking, and laughing. Whenever I would elbow my way through the crowd looking for someone, I'd get pushed and shoved around, often getting my butt squeezed by some stranger's hand. Despite my sexuality, it made me very nervous because they were drunk and older and something about it felt unpredictable and too wild for me.

One of my other jobs at the hotel was delivering finished laundry to a guest's room. Because of the pitch of my voice, often a woman would answer the door scantily dressed, thinking I was a girl, or a man barely dressed, also thinking I was a girl. One of the guests, the well-known actor Guy Kibbee, was perhaps the cheapest guest I encountered, only tipping me five cents, whereas the others usually tipped at least a quarter, sometimes even a half-dollar.

In April of that year, President Roosevelt died, and the funeral was held on a Saturday. Radios were placed in the hotel lobby to broadcast the event, and the few guests who entered that morning whispered when approaching the reception desk. I was too young to understand the impact of the president's death, but the atmosphere was eerie. I can still remember the gravitas of the hushed hotel lobby and the quiet that seemed to fall over the whole city and country that weekend as people collectively mourned.

I grew up a lot at that job, mostly due to my proximity to the adult world, but also because I learned responsibility and how to interact with many different types of people. But, as they say, all good things must come to an end. One Saturday afternoon, Mother's best friend came striding in to meet friends for lunch. Having no idea I worked there, upon seeing me in my uniform in the lobby, she grabbed my arm and pulled me to the reception desk, demanding to speak to the manager. When he came out of his office, in a voice that carried over the entire lobby, she yelled, "This boy is only thirteen years old, and it is against the law for him to be working here!"

At that, the manager took me into his office and explained he was sorry, but he had to let me go. Shamefully, I slunk into the employee locker room to change clothes, upon which a bellman asked why I was leaving. I burst out sobbing, telling him what had transpired, and how I'd lost my first real job. I was only thirteen years old, after all.

About a year later, in 1946, my mother became pregnant, and my life took another turn. Six weeks after giving birth to my sister Judy, Mother suffered a nervous breakdown. The psychiatric wards were filled with returning servicemen suffering from the traumatic effects of World War II, so she remained at home for three days and nights until a bed opened for her. She barely slept, and I remember her loudly singing and talking, which I could hear through the wall of my bedroom. To take refuge from the chaos surrounding me, I stayed in my room reading a lesbian novel, *The Well of Loneliness*. The title was appropriate because I felt so helpless and alone. How in the world did I get that book? I have no idea.

There's a certain degree of black humor in every situation, and in this instance, it was the arrival of my Orthodox Jewish grandmother. My sweet grandmother Toby traveled from her home in St. Paul to see her sick daughter, help with the cooking, and take care of the new baby. Deeply Orthodox, she arrived replete with two sets of dishes—one for milk products and the other for meat.

Upon entering my mother's bedroom, the first thing grandmother heard was Mother singing the Christian hymn "Yes, Jesus Loves Me," interspersed with vulgar expletives. My poor devout grandmother almost fainted.

After a few more days, my mother was accepted into the state mental hospital in Faribault, Minnesota, and officially diagnosed with manic depression (later called bipolar), a mental disorder we didn't know nearly as much about back then as we do today.

It was at that point that my other grandmother, Celia, came to help with the household chores and attend to the newborn baby. This grandmother, my father's mother, was the total opposite of Grandma Toby. She was a version of the stage and screen character Auntie Mame assuming the role of nurse. She had purchased a nurse's uniform which she wore with a mask. Every gesture she made was theatrical, and the way she picked up the baby to change her diaper or give her a bottle made it appear as if she were one of those robotic mannequins in a shop window. At one point, she looked at Sandy and me and said, "You know, your mother had an abortion before this one came along."

Naturally, we were stunned. Not only at the idea of our mother having had that taboo procedure but hearing the word "abortion." We later found out mother had had a miscarriage, not an abortion. Grandma Celia was nothing if not *exaggerated*.

After two weeks, Dad decided it would be a good idea if we all went to the Faribault hospital to see Mother. Just going to a mental hospital was scary for Sandy and me, but the worst part was when we were escorted into Mother's room. There we saw a shocking sight we never forgot. Our mother was drugged and strapped down to a single bed. Her flimsy nightgown had fallen open, exposing much of her naked body. She had been biting her parched lips and there was dried blood on her mouth. Sandy and I started sobbing from seeing our mother like this and ran out of the room. What could Dad have been thinking?

It became too much of a responsibility for Grandmother Celia to continue caring for the baby, so family welfare sent a woman to come help out each day. For the initial interview, a tall woman arrived wearing a big floppy felt hat which she continued to wear during the entire interview. Sandy and I sat with Dad while she explained her prior work experience. Pleased with her history, we were all smiles and delighted to know Judy would be well taken care of, but then she said there was one thing she had to show us before Dad decided to hire her. She slowly removed her hat to reveal a bald head and explained that she had had a childhood illness which had resulted in a complete loss of all her hair. Our mouths dropped open, but Dad assured her she was welcome. Lucky for us, she was an absolute delight. Not only did she take care of baby Judy, but she also tried to give us kids the warmth and love we were missing from our hospitalized and illness-stricken mother.

I suppose that's when I began dedicating more extended hours to practicing the piano. It became my sole refuge, where a single note, a measure of music, or an entire composition offered a fresh opportunity to escape from dwelling on what was happening to my mother.

It was also during that time when I began to actively explore my teenage sexuality. Still largely confused, I experienced something unsettling after seeing Montgomery Clift in the film *Red River*. I always liked going to the movies alone, sitting in a darkened theater, and ignoring the outside world. The day I watched Clift on the big screen, I began to shake all over and could barely breathe. When I left the theater, I felt like I'd crossed an invisible line I still didn't fully understand.

Then, one afternoon a few months later, in the downtown public library men's room, a man performed fellatio on me, and I liked it. My hormones were raging, and I had been an eager and willing participant, returning time after time. It felt like the perfect escape from my life at home, and a portal to a world I wanted to know more about. In a matter of a year, I had gone from a scared kid to a deeply curious and precocious young man. However, there remained the question of how to navigate my sexual feelings toward boys and my emotional attachment toward girls. One was going to be an easier, softer route in life, but that logic didn't stand a chance whenever I was in a sexual situation.

Mother finally came home after having had shock treatments for her breakdown. Even though she hadn't regained all her lost memory from those terrible treatments, our family humor was once again reinstated with me, the jackass, asking her at the dinner table, "Okay, Mom, what's my name?"

Her perpetual patience and kindness, even under these circumstances, was undimmed.

"Larry, that's enough," she replied. "Now finish your dinner and go to the piano."

I loved my mother even more for that and realized *yes, she was home.*

My musical ability progressed at a rapid pace, and I found myself obsessively practicing more difficult pieces. I relished the challenge and the struggle of learning new music, but I loved mastering a technically difficult piece more than anything in the world. At fifteen years old, I was invited to play the Mozart Coronation concerto with musicians from my high school orchestra and the Minneapolis Symphony Orchestra, under the direction of the renowned conductor, Dimitri Mitropoulos. During the final rehearsal, all went smoothly, and I was wholeheartedly congratulated by the conductor.

That evening, my proud parents were in the audience with some contraption to record my performance. I sat at the piano waiting and listening as the orchestra played the introduction to the concerto. The cellos and violins began, and I became so enthralled listening to the beautiful music I almost missed my first notes. Then, during the second movement, I suddenly drew a complete blank and proceeded to improvise for a few measures until I could regain my memory. Although I thought nobody noticed my error when the piece ended, the conductor shot me a glare I'll never forget, arresting me in my seat and filling me with a momentary burst of shame. But it didn't last long. As soon as he lowered his hands, the applause was deafening, and the crowd leaped to their feet. I had faked it again.

During high school, I worked a few part-time jobs. The first was as a clerk for a relative in his liquor store and that job was an eye-opener for a kid my age. The liquor store was in a rundown part of downtown known as the Bowery, which was heavily populated by homeless people and drunks. One afternoon, a skinny old alcoholic lady came in and bought a pint of our cheapest whisky, which she promptly tucked into the neckline of the flimsy dress covering her sagging bosom. "I don't want my old man to see this," she said. That's the kind of place it was.

My next job was at the Orpheum movie theater where I began working as a porter picking up cigarette butts off the floor. Then I became an usher, and a short while later Usher Captain. During my stint as a porter, a jukebox in the lobby played the latest hits and lots of jazz. I'd never heard jazz and was transfixed but a bit confused by the voice of a singer who sounded off-key. Every chance I had I would pretend to be sweeping up cigarette butts while lingering to listen to her sing. One evening, I told my dad my feelings about her singing, and he asked her name. "Billie Holiday," I said. At that, he roared with laughter, telling me she was a famous jazz singer. Although something about jazz truly excited me, my training in classical music had been so structured I was unable to let go enough to be able to play jazz myself.

In those days, famous big bands often played during the intermission of a current film. Horace Height and his Musical Knights, Count Basie and his orchestra, and Stan Kenton, featuring the singer June Christie (who sang jazz on key), were just a few who performed weekly.

Horace Height's star was a teenage accordionist named Dick Contino. Along with his co-star Debbie Dewer, Dick would invite me out for coffee after work, always asking about my progress studying the piano and playfully suggesting I join the band and play something flashy such as De Falla's "Ritual Fire Dance." It sounded like a good idea, but Mr. Height wasn't the least bit interested so it never happened.

My last part-time job was at Merrill Lynch, Fenner & Beane, where I was hired as a board marker. Two of us boys stood on a small stage in front of the stockbrokers sitting at their desks. We read quotes from teletypes and quickly chalk-marked the quotes on a large blackboard. It was an exciting experience, and I learned a lot about the stock market—enough so that I even thought that when I got out of school there might be a position open for me where I could learn to be a broker. Of course, it was just a passing idea because my main interest was still the piano. Above all else, I dreamed of being a concert pianist.

I studied German in North High because much of the classical sheet music at the time was published in Leipzig, Germany, and the notations on the sheet music were in German. In our German class, each student was assigned a pen pal in a school located in the Russian-German zone. My pen pal was a boy my age to whom I wrote in German, and who would write to me in English. Little by little, his letters became less frequent and filled with tales of food rationing and deprivation, until the last one when he said the letters would soon have to be smuggled out. Shortly after that, the Russians closed the border and all correspondence ceased. I've often wondered about that boy and what might have become of him.

My life was that of a typical American teenager, except when we boys would double-date. In one of my friend's cars, we would take our girlfriends to the movies or canoeing on Lake of the Isles. The girls we dated were nice, pristine virgins who weren't known for "putting out," so after our evening together we'd take them home and then we boys, stimulated by the evening, would go somewhere and masturbate together. We'd heard of the Polish boys on the East side of town doing something called "corn holing" (anal sex), but we considered that very low class because, after all, we did have our standards.

I discovered I'd broken one, however, when I told my best friend Raymond that I had met a sailor in a movie theater. I never told him of any other encounters I'd had, but I felt this one was special, so I confided in him. (I was so naive that after that sexual encounter with the sailor, I told him the next time he was on leave he might like to come to my parents' house for dinner.)

"What? You did it with a sailor?" he said. "A *stranger?*"

I guess it was considered okay to be sexually involved with a friend, but not with a stranger.

You could say I was more or less living the life of a normal teen—going to school, hanging out with friends, having girlfriends, finding time to continue practicing the piano, reading books, and doing what kids usually do. There were tough times, but I found a way to stay optimistic despite it all, and that's one of the great gifts I was given by my mom. Under different circumstances, I could have easily ended up leading a less fulfilling life, yet even in the face of poverty, mental health challenges, and enduring emotional abuse from my father, I always knew that I would eventually overcome it all.

I knew there was a big world out there waiting for me.

The apartment across from Sumner Field enabled me to luxuriate in my love of ice skating. When I discovered my school friend Morty was a good skater, we spent many a winter evening figure skating under the park lights, innocently holding hands, and going around and around the sparkling rink, totally oblivious to the other skaters and fantasizing about running away from home to join the Ice Follies. It may not have been a love affair, but there was love in the air between us, and we didn't have a care in the world or any concern whatsoever about what the other skaters on that frozen pond might think. Out there, it was just the two of us and our big feelings and dreams for the future. All these years later, on a crisp, cold night, I can still get transported to that time and feel the magic in the air.

The renowned Polish-American pianist Arthur Rubinstein was my musical hero, and in my junior year, he happened to be coming to town to perform with the Minneapolis Symphony Orchestra. I thought going to the concert would be my only chance, ever, to hear him in person, so I decided to skip school and attend the matinee performance.

I got there early with enough time to wander around and explore the building. At the rear, I noticed the stage door half-open and decided to walk in. A guard immediately stopped me, gruffly asking what I wanted. I said I was the president of the Arthur Rubinstein Fan Club and that I would like to get his autograph. (There was no Arthur Rubinstein Fan Club that I was aware of.) The conductor, Dimitri Mitropolous, spotted me standing there and immediately came over to see what I was doing. As I stammered an explanation, he smiled, and at that moment I was sure he recognized me from playing with our school's symphony orchestra or from nights at the Bowery's Bijou movie theater, a place where he and I had cruised for sex alongside each other but never with each other.

He sent the guard away, saying it was okay for me to get the autograph since I was, after all, the president of the fan club. Then, laughing, he took me by the hand and led me down a hall to a dressing room where he introduced me to my idol, Arthur Rubinstein, who, in turn, led me into another room with a piano where he invited me to sit down and play something for him.

I was incredibly nervous. As I sat at the piano, my knees shook so badly I could barely keep my foot on the sustaining pedal. Shortly after I began to play, a man rushed in saying the room was not soundproof and they could hear me in the auditorium and out in the halls. Even though the concert hadn't yet begun, I had to stop playing for my hero and the adventure came to a halt just as quickly as it had started.

I'd only played for a few minutes, but Rubinstein graciously offered a critique anyway, saying my technique had been good. He'd even noticed that I'd been trained in the Russian style of curved fingers hitting the keys like little hammers, just as he had been. A photographer from the local newspaper came in to photograph Rubinstein and, seeing the two of us, took pictures of us together: me sitting at the piano and Rubinstein leaning on it as if he were still listening to me playing.

After the photographs, I thanked Mr. Rubinstein and made my way out. An usher said he had a seat for me in the front row. Shortly after I sat down, the orchestra took their seats and began playing Borodin's "In the Steppes of Central Asia." Sitting there basking in my contact with Rubinstein, in a beautiful concert hall all by myself in the front row, I felt as though I were floating on air. The events of the day had been much more than I ever would have imagined, and I couldn't wait to tell my parents.

As soon as I could find a telephone booth after the concert, I called my mother, excitedly telling her I had just met and played for Arthur Rubinstein. Unimpressed by the importance of the encounter and unfamiliar with his name, she demanded, "Why aren't you in school?" As Mother always said, she knew nothing of "that kind" of music. Sandy and I would tease her by asking, "Mother, who wrote Greig's 'A Minor Concerto'?" She'd just shake her head and walk away.

She would understand what a big deal it was soon enough. Lo and behold, on the front page of the next morning's newspaper was the photograph. There I was for all the world to see: a long-haired sixteen-year-old in my faded plaid cotton shirt with the one and only

Arthur Rubinstein! That was my second time in the newspaper, the first as a shop owner in kindergarten, and now as a classical pianist playing for my idol. I walked into school that morning a hero to my friends but a liability to the principal. He said even though he and the faculty were proud of me, I was never to skip school again. But meeting my idol had been worth it, for sure.

At some point during my mid-teens, as a diversion from playing the piano, I began designing women's dresses. I would kneel on the living room floor painstakingly copying illustrations of models wearing dresses sold in Young and Quinlan, the most prestigious department store in town (in those days there were no photo ads). Then, after mastering the copy, I would draw a figure with my own dress design, such as a slim floor-length white crêpe de chine with long sleeves and a round neck, all the while imagining it would be worn by the actress Lizabeth Scott, a favorite of mine with her long blonde hair and deep voice. Many years later I would meet Scott at a party and tell her of my childhood admiration, saying how flattered she was that she had been my muse. But back on the floor in Minneapolis, with my sketchbook and pencils and magazines, the world of high fashion was still a remote daydream.

One day, I noticed an ad in the newspaper for a Design-a-Blouse contest sponsored by Powers department store. I wanted to win the contest, but I didn't dare enter a submission under my name. Boys didn't design women's clothes in those days—at least not in Minnesota. Yet I refused to concede defeat. I sketched a simple blouse and submitted it anyway, using the first name "Lorraine" in my cover letter and return address. A few weeks later, I received a packet in the mail, which I'd been on the lookout for every day since sending it off. I'd won an honorable mention and a yearlong subscription to the store's magazine, *Butchy's Business*.

That was easy enough, I thought. Here I'd been practicing the piano for hours on end every day, and in a fraction of the time it took to learn a piece of music, I was able to place in a competition as a designer. That experience was the first time I thought that maybe there was another world out there for me aside from playing the piano. As far-fetched as it once had seemed, maybe there was a way for a kid like me to become a designer after all. But that thought stayed in the back of my mind as I continued working toward a career as a concert pianist.

One day, while browsing through a fashion magazine Mother had brought home from the beauty parlor, I stopped dead in my tracks seeing an ad for Diorama cologne by Christian Dior. It was a sketch of a woman's face by someone with one name, GRAU. The lines were bold, and I began to incorporate that method of sketching in my designs. Ironically, neither of my parents commented on my sketching, spoke to me of my newfound interest, or encouraged me to pursue it as a career. In retrospect, I doubt my parents even knew what a dress designer was, let alone how to guide their child to become one.

In that same magazine, I also read an article about the latest Paris collection by Christian Dior. He'd shown what was sensationally called the "New Look," and the designs were quickly being copied by manufacturers in the United States. Soon after, as luck would have it, my father's very rich aunt invited Dad and me to lunch. She picked us up in her navy-blue Chrysler Town and Country station wagon wearing one of those copied designs. Seeing it in person was a revelation—that a trendy design could go from the runway in Paris to Minneapolis, Minnesota felt as if it had leaped from the pages of the magazine and into real life. Something about that thrilled me. I loved feeling like I was in the know and on the cutting edge of trendy fashion, and once again, my thoughts turned to becoming a designer.

Mother began suffering from more mental problems, and every time the telephone rang in a classroom I tensed, thinking I might be called home again. At this point, I was a senior in high school, and what with Dad working the night shift at Honeywell and Mother in and out of the hospital, I had no supervision. For the first time in my life, I was free to come and go as I wished. I began to run wild, staying out all night and associating with all kinds of gay people.

One night, I stayed over at the apartment of a man I'd met. When I returned home very early the next morning, Dad was waiting. He angrily confronted me about my behavior, saying he knew I had been staying out late. He grabbed my wrist and warned me that if I didn't behave, he was going to call the "gun squad." (In his anger, he referenced a term from his own Boston childhood that meant the police)—the silver ID bracelet I was wearing broke and fell to the floor. I stared at him for a long moment, then turned and defiantly slammed the door to my room. The quiet kid I had been was no more. From then on, my dad and I rarely spoke to one another.

I quickly became more aggressive in flaunting my sexuality, even though I still hadn't fully figured it out. The corner of 7th Street and Hennepin Avenue in downtown Minneapolis was where I always caught my bus home, and it was at that corner where an important part of my teen life played out. Too young to get into the gay bar down the street, I hung out with other gay boys my age, laughing and pretending we were dating the men we saw going into that bar.

On one of those evenings, I was wearing my new green and white satin Vikings club jacket, waiting for the bus, when a car pulled over and the driver offered me a ride home. He was very handsome, twenty-something years old, and invited me back to his apartment, an offer I readily accepted. As soon as we arrived, he offered me a glass of apple brandy. I had never had liquor and was immediately tipsy, and then one thing led to another. We saw each other again and after our third encounter, he told me he was the choir director at St. Olaf's College—and that he loved me.

Startled by his comment, I said, "Men don't love men." I loved the sex, but I still had no idea that it was possible for men to love men outside of the bedroom. Plus, he'd been so eager and forward with his confession of love that it turned me off. I felt pressured to reciprocate his feelings and I couldn't, so the director and I stopped seeing each other after that and I continued sowing my oats, as they say.

It was on that same corner where other unexpected encounters transpired. Once, after attending the Ice Follies show, I was standing on the corner when a good-looking man approached asking me for directions to the Radisson Hotel. I told him I'd once worked there and would show him the way. When we arrived, he invited me up to his room, and in the elevator, I realized he was a star skater with the Follies I'd just seen! As soon as we were in his room, things got heavy quickly and, being with a star, I was completely smitten.

I went back to the hotel the following day to drop off a note telling him I'd like to stay in touch. The same moment I stepped out of the revolving door into the hotel lobby, the skater, along with two other men, were stepping into the revolving door, on their way out of the hotel. I started to say hello, but he brushed past me, pretending I was a stranger.

I was crushed. That night, I cried in my bed with the autographed photo of the skater lying beside me. It was my first rejection.

I managed not to let the disappointment keep me down, though. As a fledgling gay person, still closeted and confused, I had to find ways to express myself without blowing my cover. I continued to date girls, at least until I could graduate. Being gay in the Midwest at that time, even in a larger city like Minneapolis, wasn't desirable in the least. But you find a way. You must, otherwise what's the alternative? Deprivation? Living a lie? That seemed bleak, so I learned how to "pass" in the straight world while discreetly exploring other parts of my sexuality that were yearning to come out. I couldn't yet bring myself to understand how two men could be in a relationship or spend a life together. I had no models and therefore no clue it was even possible.

The Jewel Box Revue was a well-known drag show that had come to Minneapolis from Miami. It was staged in a downtown nightclub just up the street from my usual bus stop. One evening, while waiting for the bus, I walked over to look at the photos of the performers displayed in the window. I had never seen anything like men in women's clothes, and I was fascinated. As I stood there, the door to the club opened and a well-dressed older man came out. He asked if I would like to see the show. I explained I was only seventeen, and he said as long as I was a guest of his and didn't drink liquor, I was welcome. He turned out to be Doc Benner, the owner of the revue.

We walked in and sat down at a front table, and he ordered me a Coke. The show began and all the performers lip-synced to recorded music—except for one, TC Jones. TC was the star of the show and sang in a woman's voice until the end of his act when he bowed and pulled off his wig, revealing a bald head. I was shocked. When the show was over, TC and another performer came to the table to sit with us, immediately asking who I was and why was I there. During the conversation, I mentioned I was studying to be a concert pianist. TC asked if I could also write out music because he wanted to sing a new song called "Lush Life," but there was only a recording by Nat King Cole and no sheet music available.

"Sure," I said, "it's easy." He said that if I could listen to the record and then transcribe the song, he would pay me. I immediately agreed, thinking, *Wow, nobody has ever paid me for anything like this.* I took the recording home that night and began listening to it over and over again, writing out all of the notes.

Whenever I had the chance, I went back to the club and soon became friendly with many other performers. In many ways, I became their "mascot," and they became my guardian angels. Looking back, I marvel at how willing and adventurous I was. To this day, I'm so grateful for those performers and for the kindness of Doc Benner, who saw something in me that he knew needed protection. Without them, I would have missed out on so much of my sexual maturity. They made it okay for me to be who I was by giving me a safe place to work through all my confusion and exploration, and they showed me how to have a good time.

One evening, one of the drag performers, Riki Renee, thought it would be fun to take me to my first gay party. I had no idea what to expect, imagining all sorts of sordid things. The party was held in someone's house and the first thing I saw when we walked in was one of my mother's closest friends with her arm around another woman. Immediately, my thoughts went to my mother. Was she a lesbian too? Should I leave?

Then the woman spotted me standing there and blurted out, "Your mother knows nothing about this. Just pretend you didn't see me." To reassure me, she kissed my cheek and introduced me to her lady friend. As I wandered around a bit dazed, a Black woman walked up to me saying she remembered me coming to her church on Lyndale and seeing my little white face poking up against that screen door.

I felt wonderful being there among people who understood me, so wonderful that I proceeded to get roaring drunk for the first time in my life, eventually passing out on a couch.

After that, I returned night after night to the club, flattered by the attention I was getting from all the performers. But it wasn't all as rosy as I first thought. One evening, I stayed until the bar closed and planned to walk all the way home because the bus had stopped running at that late hour. Doc said that since we were having so much fun, we should keep the party going in his hotel room. Naively thinking there would be others arriving, I went with him to his room, and he quickly attempted to undress me. I tried pulling my clothes on and getting to the door but he kept struggling with me.

I finally yelled, "If you don't let me go, I'll scream for the house detective."

At that, he released me, admitting that he was drunk. He said he was sorry and offered to drive me home, pleading with me not to mention it to anyone. I swore I wouldn't, and we got into his car. At that time, people drove drunk a lot more than they would today, and I didn't think twice about taking a ride from him in that state. Just goes to show how much things change over time. In the car, he repeatedly apologized, going so far as to offer to return later that morning and drive me to school so I could sleep in and not have to walk there.

I took him up on it, and by morning, I'd let the whole matter go. Doc was an honest man and had been good to me that year, and I knew anyone was prone to making a mistake when they were drunk. Plus, he'd stopped when I'd asked him to, and it wasn't like it was a regular occurrence. My first class that morning was with my music teacher, Mrs. Etscheid, who'd made a serious impression on me a year prior when she'd arrived at our school wearing a Molyneux-designed suit and sporting a big marquis-cut diamond on her wedding finger. I'd overheard someone say she'd directed the choir at the Metropolitan Opera in New York and was always curious why she came to teach at our lowly North High. She was very strict about the way she taught, forcefully clapping her hands beating out the music tempo. In class, we often discussed different kinds of music and on this day, she asked me to tell the class what I was currently studying on the piano. It was a piece by Debussy, and too nervous to say *"La Plus Que Lente"* in front of the class in proper French, I said it in phonetic English instead. She then had me come up in front of the class and repeat the name in French. When I did, all she said was, "Back your convictions!" And that was advice I never forgot because whenever I did, things didn't go well.

When class ended that morning, Mrs. Etscheid asked me to stay after the rest of the students had left. I had no idea why, but after closing the door she invited me to sit closer to her, saying she had a delicate subject to discuss. In a soft voice, she said she had seen me getting out of a white Lincoln Continental with Florida license plates that morning. I blushed, and she continued to say that if that was the life I wished to lead, she wanted me to know there were nicer people out there than the man who had dropped me off. That was all. Nothing more. Thanking her, I left the room a bit bewildered, trying to absorb her seemingly kind advice and reconcile my newly complicated feelings about a man whom I thought had been good to me—for the most part, anyway.

Such were the strange happenings of my adolescence: close calls with danger, strangers acting benevolent one day and unsafe the next, and a random assortment of unexpected people looking after me in one way or another.

Spring came, and along with it, prom and graduation day. When the prom approached and the other students were scrambling for dates, I had neither the money nor the interest to attend. Instead, I spent the evening in the bar with my Jewel Box Revue friends, a decision I have never regretted.

Graduation itself was an event my schoolmates and their families celebrated together, but, unfortunately, my parents were not around. In my cap and gown, I celebrated alone. Mother was in another mental hospital and Dad was sleeping days and working nights. I was just happy leaving a school where I felt I had little in common with my fellow students. After all, I was a serious classical piano student and they only wanted to party.

Was I lonely during this time? I don't know. I had my friends at the Jewel Box Review, I had my music and my fashion illustrations, and I still went to the movies, happy to be sitting there alone without any thoughts of my dysfunctional life at home and my confusing existence. The World Theater was the only theater in town that showed foreign films, usually the very English J. Arthur Rank productions, and I often sat there thinking about who among my friends would understand my attraction to movies like *The Red Shoes*, *Brief Encounter*, and *Dead of Night*.

Walking home from the theater at night, I would sometimes feel slightly frightened. To allay those fears, I softly sang a French song I'd heard on the radio sung by Hildegarde, a well-known chanteuse. The song was *J'attendrai*, and somehow, this song soothed me like none other. The English translation "I Will Wait" was a perfect caption for my life at the time because, without knowing it, I was indeed waiting for something—I just had no idea what it was.

In short order, I graduated high school, my part-time job at Merrill Lynch became full-time, and I started living the day-by-day existence of a grown-up. My parents had given me no direction about what to do upon graduating other than "get a job." Nobody had told me how to apply for or obtain college scholarships, and I had never really thought about going to one anyway. I still studied the piano and hung out at night on that street corner downtown, but I was starting to worry that I was quickly slipping into a boring adult life in Minnesota.

That is, until one evening, as I was leaning on a metal rail at my usual 7th and Hennepin bus stop, a kid about my age walked up to me and, in a low sultry voice said, "Well, hello there. My name is Frank— what's yours?"

Here before me stood a young man with the shiniest black hair I'd ever seen, shaded green eyes, full red lips, and translucent pale skin. We stood there chatting and then, suddenly, he pushed himself up to sit on the rail. I grabbed his arms to keep him from falling over into the deep stairwell behind, and it was then that our eyes met.

That was the beginning of my first love affair with another male. I was seventeen years old.

Frank Hill's father was the commissioner of health for the State of Minnesota, and his mother, a beauty resembling the actress Hedy Lamarr, had emigrated from Ireland and spoke with a charming Irish brogue. Frank took me to his parents' house and after meeting me for the first time, they immediately embraced his "new friend," never dreaming of our actual relationship. Or so I thought.

Frank's mother, having been told I was Jewish and thinking I might be curious, invited me to a Sunday Mass, along with her and Frank, at the Catholic cathedral in St. Paul. Sandy and I had always been told by our father to visit other denominations' churches and listen to what they had to say, but to always remember we were Jewish. With that thought in mind, and since I never had been to a Catholic church, I decided to attend the Mass.

The three of us sat in a pew listening to the priest's sermon—until he started saying the Jews had killed Christ. At that, Mrs. Hill grabbed my arm and dragged me out of the place. That night, Frank and I decided to get our revenge. We took the streetcar to St. Paul and in the dark proceeded to engage in a sexual act on the steps leading into the grand cathedral. It was perverse and wonderful.

We were madly in love, but our relationship was difficult because we were too young to have a private place to be alone together. One evening, Frank and I were invited to a party at the house of an older man who befriended underage boys, and as I wandered through the house, I was led down into the basement by another young boy who began to kiss me. Frank walked in and, seeing me kissing somebody else, rushed back up the stairs, shouting that he never wanted to see me again. I begged him to reconsider, but he refused and ran out the door.

Despondent, I began to walk home by way of a bridge that crossed over the Mississippi River. When I got to the middle, I stopped and looked over at the chunks of ice rushing past in the dark water, wondering if I should kill myself since I could no longer be with Frank. My next thought was, what if I hit the ice? I'll only hurt myself, not drown. My third thought was: here I am wearing a new gray flannel spring coat, wouldn't it be a shame to ruin it?

My lucky angels took over and I hailed a passing taxi, went to Frank's house, quietly knocked on his bedroom window, climbed into bed with him, pleaded my case, and then, after reconciling and cuddling all night, left at dawn.

Today, I can say, without reservation, that fashion saved my life that night. Or maybe it was pride. Either way, that gray flannel coat kept me alive. Little did I know at the time that it was the first of many important moments that fashion would play in my life.

Still banging away at the piano for as many hours as I could spare each day after work, I finally realized that although I was a very good pianist, I wasn't great, and to be a concert pianist one had to be great. I remembered the design contest I'd won and how much it had excited me, so I decided to start researching schools in New York where I could learn design. How I was going to do that since I had no money and had never heard of a scholarship, I didn't know, but the idea of New York thrilled me, and I just knew I would find a way.

My mother's sister Ethel lived in New York. Whenever she visited, she told us enticing stories of visiting museums, attending Broadway shows, and going on shopping expeditions, all of which made me more determined to move to that exciting city. I just hadn't put it together until after I'd graduated high school. And with all the stuff going on at home, it was never a serious option until then.

Also, my father's uncle had come to Minneapolis to appear in *Diamond Lil* with Mae West and he, too, told stories about living in the city. So, I began doing research, studying a map to become familiar with the places they spoke of, and memorizing all the streets and how they intersected. New York became my great obsession.

Two friends had moved there from Minneapolis and when they wrote and invited me to stay with them, that did it! I discussed my decision with my best friend Raymond and, understanding my burning desire to leave, he convinced his wealthy parents to give me an airplane ticket as a gift for my eighteenth birthday. His parents agreed and gave me a one-way Northwest Airlines ticket.

With the gift in hand, I told my parents of my decision and they readily agreed. The night before I left, Dad took me aside to give me this sage advice: "If a prostitute approaches you, just kick her in the you-know-what." With that ill-advised warning and wearing my Prince of Wales plaid suit (pants and sleeves lengthened), I waved goodbye to my parents and boarded the plane, taking my assigned aisle seat.

As we lifted off and Minneapolis grew smaller and smaller beneath us, I had the distinct feeling that my adult life had officially begun.

FOUR

New York, New York

The plane landed at LaGuardia Airport, where I was met by my aunt. In the taxi, as we zoomed across town to her Manhattan apartment on Riverside Drive, I immediately felt electricity in the air. New York City was buzzing, and so was I. I'd made it to the city I'd always dreamed of.

At her building, we were promptly greeted by two doormen. Then, two elevator men! She introduced me to each one and told them they would be seeing a great deal of me in the future, but since my living arrangement was to be on 23rd Street and 3rd Avenue, I bid adieu to my aunt and, with subway instructions and suitcase in hand, traversed across town to move in with my two friends.

The following evening, my friends took me to Times Square. Lights were blazing, the Camel cigarette sign blowing smoke into the night sky, and I could barely catch my breath as I tried to take it all in. On the way back to the apartment, I innocently asked what the big building was that looked like a Pepsi bottle.

"That's the Empire State Building, dumb hick," my friend Billy said.

My first small-town-boy-in-the-big-city mistake. The first of many, though aside from some expected rookie mistakes, I like to think I caught on rather quickly to the cosmopolitan way of life.

Before leaving Minneapolis, I had taken the precaution of asking for a letter of recommendation from Merrill Lynch. Since I had a good reference, I thought I'd be able to land a job at their location in the Wall Street district, so I found the address in the phone book and took the subway to 70 Pine Street. I was immediately hired as a Runner, carrying securities from one brokerage house to another. With very little money, I asked for an advance on my salary of thirty-five dollars a week so I could find a place to live on my own. To my delight, they agreed.

With my first week's check advance, I moved into a studio apartment in an old, converted mansion on 73rd Street between Columbus and Amsterdam Avenues. An enormous marble fireplace practically filled the room. A few weeks later, I received a letter from Frank Hill, who informed me he was going to run away from home to join me in New York. Frank was only sixteen and impetuous. I had no idea how we would live on my meager salary, but I was excited to see him. I wrote him back immediately and told him to come as soon as he could.

Rain or shine, I delivered securities every day, not only to other brokerage houses but also to individuals and other organizations. I once saw a security with my uncle's name on it; another time, I delivered a million-dollar check to Mr. Beane himself (he was a partner at the firm) at his home on Sutton Place. At night and on the weekends, I explored everything the city had to offer, marveling at the elegant architecture and the way people strode along the sidewalks with confidence and purpose. I loved the way they dressed, too, and I often found myself idly wandering the streets, window shopping outside all the great department stores of the day.

Soon after arriving in the city, Frank took a job dressing windows at Ohrbach's department store, which helped financially. During that time, we were introduced to Sam Anderson, about ten years our senior, who was a pianist at the upscale bar and restaurant Number One Fifth Avenue. When he heard about our tight living arrangement, he said he had a one-bedroom apartment he laughingly called a "garden apartment" on 75th Street just off Broadway that he would be happy to share with us. (The basement apartment had never seen the light of day.) Frank and I could share it, sleeping on twin sofas in the living room, and Sam would continue sleeping in the bedroom. It might not sound like an upgrade, but it was. We were tripping over each other in my studio, so we moved into Sam's place, painted the walls pink, and reupholstered the sofas with gray fabric Frank had stolen from his job. Everything was stapled together just like he did in the windows at Ohrbach's. Our budget was eight dollars a week each for dinner, and at the end of the week that left us, the happy couple, with one dollar each, which we invariably spent on a Saturday night out, usually on a drink in the Oak Room at the glamorous Plaza Hotel.

The Oak Room bar was always six-deep with gay men. Being young and "presentable," me in my old suit and Frank in a blue blazer, we were regularly offered drinks by other patrons. One evening, when we decided to try something different and went for hamburgers instead at P. J. Clarke's, a renowned bar we'd read about, the bartender took one look at us and said, "Your bars are down the street, not here." He meant the three gay bars on the East Side known as the "Bird Circuit." We fled, ashamed, and vowed to never set foot in a place like P. J. Clarke's again.

On the Saturday night before Easter, we were invited to an

Easter Hat Party, for which we were to create our own Easter hats to wear at the party. I thought I would design something special for myself, so I went to a pet store and bought a few little yellow baby chicks and some chicken wire. When I got home, I took one of Sam's silver serving trays, put the baby chicks on it, covered the tray with chicken wire, and decorated the whole thing with fake flowers. A big blue ribbon, which I tied snugly beneath, finished it off.

Upon entering the party, the little chicks gaily chirped, as if on cue, and the hat was a sensation. However, as soon as I turned my head, the tray tilted, and chicken poop spilled out onto my shoulders, forcing me to carry the hat for the entire evening. My only suit jacket was nearly ruined, but the hat won first prize for Most Creative.

Leaving the party a bit tipsy, I carried the hat out to the street while Frank hailed a taxi. Just as I was about to get in, I tripped on the curb, dropping the hat. The chicks escaped the broken chicken wire and ran out all over the Madison Avenue sidewalk. We chased after them while the cab driver and a couple of bystanders laughed hysterically. We finally managed to get them all back in the hat, and once we got home, I figured the bathtub would be the safest place to keep them overnight. So, I put them in there, shut the door, and went to bed.

All night long, we heard the chirp chirp chirping, keeping us wide awake and even, at one point, waking up Sam. The next morning, realizing it was Easter Sunday and that the pet shop where I had intended to return the damn things would be closed, I put them in a box, walked over to nearby Central Park, and let the tiny chicks run free. Frank was furious with me for leaving those small chicks in the park, and those chicks' great grand chicks are probably in the park to this day.

It was a wonderful time in my life, away from home for the first time and taking advantage of the big city. It felt like I was finally growing up and becoming a part of the world. But city life was tough, especially on a tight budget and in a cramped space with a volatile boyfriend like Frank. We argued and fought all the time, usually about not having enough money and rarely having any alone time. On occasion, Frank would become violent, pick me up and throw me onto one of the sofas, and then jump on top of me, grabbing my neck to choke me. Each time, I would fight him off, but we'd be so wound up that we'd go to bed angry with one another. I can't imagine either of us slept at all those nights, I just remember staring at the ceiling wondering how things could ever be any different than they were right then. New York City wasn't the problem, but our living conditions together became unbearable and, as if one of those late-night prayers had been answered, Frank's parents asked him to come back home. We both knew it was for the best, even though we'd given it our all, and so he returned.

With Frank gone, I was free to explore New York alone again, visiting shops, museums, and a few concerts at Carnegie Hall. As much as I'd enjoyed having Frank around, in the end, it felt like I'd had a false start in the city and that I'd never really had a proper chance to experience it by myself. The Plaza Hotel still held an attraction for me, and some evenings I would go in the Fifth Avenue entrance and sit on one of the little gold chairs near the entry to the Palm Court, watching beautifully dressed guests coming and going and wishing I were one of them.

On one of those evenings, I saw a sign in the lobby with the name of a charity for children called the Milk Fund and a ballroom number. *Why not?* I thought, and walked to the elevator, taking it up to the second floor. When the elevator door opened, I spotted a woman sitting at the desk in front of the entrance to the dining room.

"Name, please," she asked.

Without thinking twice, I said, "Bill Robertson," pulling it out of thin air and hoping it was generic and common enough to be on the list.

She nodded and began thumbing through a box holding tickets as I stood there waiting and smiling. And then, the miracle of miracles.

"Here you are, Mr. Robertson," she said, handing me a ticket.

I immediately thought: *Now what do I do?* I walked into the large dining room, looked around at the glamorous people, turned, and fled.

As fate would have it, on Monday morning, as I exited the subway and walked to work through the graveyard beside Trinity Church, I passed a tombstone with the name of none other than Bill Robertson. I would pass this name many times thereafter and wonder if there had indeed been a guest at that benefit with the same name or if that woman at the registration table was just being nice to me. In any event, the ghost of Bill Robertson played some kind of role in my life, even though I had been unaware of what it was.

I continued going to the Oak Room bar but never left with anyone. Except for one evening, when a very charming older man struck up a conversation and explained he was to have met someone there, but the person became ill, and he had already booked a table at the restaurant Allegro. He asked me if I would be his date for dinner. I'd heard about the very expensive gay restaurant and never imagined I would go. He was such a nice man, and it seemed like such a wonderful opportunity, so I accepted.

We took a taxi to the restaurant where a uniformed doorman opened the door for us, and then the host led us to a table in the main dining room near the piano. Trying to be sophisticated, my head held up extra high, I tripped on the small step entering the dining room. Luckily no one aside from my "date" noticed. Once we were seated, he ordered dinner for the two of us. The pianist, Bart Howard, played the piano, and a singer named Portia Nelson stood singing a song Howard had written called "In Other Words" (which later became known as "Fly Me to the Moon"). The evening was going well until I felt the man's hand on my leg, at which point I said I felt ill and needed to go to the men's room. As nice as he'd been, I wasn't attracted to him in the least, and I didn't have it in me to sleep with anyone I wasn't attracted to. When I came out, I told him I'd thrown up and had best go home immediately. As soon as I left the restaurant, I ran across town to my apartment. Luckily, I never saw the gentleman again.

I'd found another small studio on West 52nd Street just a couple of doors from the fabled 21 Club. It was in a converted brownstone and the one public telephone was on the ground floor. Whenever the phone rang, all the studio apartment doors opened, and whoever was around ran for the phone. The building was full of delightful characters: a lovely petite hat model who worked for hat designer John Frederics, and a girdle model who worked on Seventh Avenue. Then there was Bob! A handsome blond boy from Dallas whose family paid him to stay away because he was gay. Bob couldn't have been happier to be a thousand miles from them and living in New York City. He loved the idea of there being so many available men in New York and would say to me, "Honey, I just walk out the door and down those steps and there he is. Our eyes lock, our legs lock, and away we go!" He was the kindest person. One day, seeing I was cold in my thin coat, he gave me a camel hair overcoat. Not just to borrow, but to keep. Yes, there were numerous young men in New York whose families had disowned them. I'd see some in limousines with older men, but I knew that wasn't the life I wanted. The life I wanted was still vaguely in the back of my mind, and it involved making it on my own merits and talent.

Each Wednesday, I dutifully called my parents "collect" at a certain hour. That was the code for them to refuse to take my call, hang up the phone, and then quickly call me back, which was cheaper. On one of those Wednesdays, Mother called back and promptly informed me they were moving to California the following Saturday. I sputtered and asked about my piano and my record collection. How did this happen? And how could they just up and move without even consulting me? I was told most of my things had been given away, my piano had been sold, and that it was a split-second decision because they were tired of the cold and snow in January and Dad being ill all the time. They were going to live in Venice in a house my aunt Sally had found for them. Given a few more details, I angrily hung up the phone and cried.

As badly as I had wanted to escape Minneapolis, I'd never considered the idea that I might not be able to return and enjoy the familiar comforts of my childhood home again. It felt like a crushing blow. It felt personal. And there was absolutely nothing I could do about it.

Three months later, my military draft notice arrived, stating the date and place in downtown New York where I was to be interviewed. During the interview, the sergeant asked if I'd ever had homosexual relations. Not knowing what to say, I blurted out that I had, but one time only. A lie, of course. The interviewer said that was a normal occurrence among young men. As soon as I got the notice, I'd had Mother send me a file of letters from doctors attesting to having fractured my vertebrae in a ski accident when I was seventeen. I figured that was certainly enough to disqualify me from service. The doctor took the file and attached it to my application, but I could tell by his expression it wasn't going to keep me out of the military.

Soon after, I quit my job with Merrill Lynch and took a train from New York to Minneapolis for a week's stay. I planned to visit our neighbors who had some of my music and other belongings and to see Frank for what was to be the last time before embarking on another long journey taking the Golden State train to Los Angeles via Chicago. I'd been in New York for just under nine months. It was bittersweet coming back to Minnesota, at once familiar with all my old haunts and friends, and yet like visiting some far-off place I used to call home, with a sense of emptiness and sadness without my family there. I'd grown up quite a bit in my short time away, and Minneapolis no longer felt like home at all.

But it was only a temporary stopover. Another adventure was going to begin, and my life was about to change in ways I'd never imagined.

FIVE

California, Here I Come

I took a long bus ride to Chicago, where I boarded the Golden State train and settled into my uncomfortable coach seat for the three-day trip to Los Angeles. I was thrilled to be going way out west for the first time. I'd long admired the Hollywood stars who I'd been keeping tabs on for years. I loved the glamour and their impeccable sense of style. And I'd always been drawn to the landscape of the West. There was something so magical about it for a kid from the landlocked Midwest. Just like New York City, California represented a world of endless possibility—the only problem being that I wasn't going there to "make it," I was going to avoid the draft!

After a long, tiring trip, the train arrived in Pasadena, California, where I saw a bright blue sunny sky silhouetted by tall palm trees. The California landscape and sunlight invigorated me, and I was suddenly no longer tired as I stood at the back of the car awaiting my destination.

Bill, my aunt Sally's boyfriend, met me at Union Station in downtown Los Angeles and drove me to my parents' rental house in

Venice. In his Buick convertible, he gave a running commentary, pointing out famous sites along Sunset Boulevard while I tried to absorb it all. Then we turned a corner and there it was! The blue Pacific Ocean sparkling in the sunshine. My body slumped and I immediately felt relaxed.

That is until I saw dismal, rundown Venice. Bill parked and we walked to the end of a short block lined with small Craftsman-style houses to my parents' house near the beach. It was rough even at first glance, and I wondered if they were truly okay living in such a shady neighborhood. This is coming from a kid who grew up in the projects, so you can imagine what shape it must have been in.

The door to the house opened and Mother came out, hugging and kissing me. She immediately saw my amazement upon entering the clapboard house. My cute little sister Judy kept looking at me as if I were a stranger. I wasn't sure she even remembered who I was. Ever the optimist, my mother said, "Larry, just pretend you are in a house at White Bear Lake in Minnesota because housing is difficult to find and we are lucky to be so close to the beach."

My parents' house was small and sleeping on the living room sofa was not very comfortable. As luck would have it, a few days later, on nearby Crystal Beach, a gay beach with bars and a bathhouse, I met a person my age looking for a roommate. His Montana Avenue apartment in Santa Monica had a small extra bedroom and was a short walk into downtown where I soon found a job at a men's clothing store.

The retail chain I worked for in Santa Monica wasn't very interesting, but it paid the bills. Each day I checked the mail with nerves fluttering in my stomach, hoping it wouldn't be the day the New York draft office would catch up with me.

Without a car, my days and nights were limited to exploring the beach city I lived in and an occasional bus ride to Hollywood. I'd heard Palm Springs mentioned a lot since I'd been in Santa Monica, so one weekend I decided to be adventuresome and hopped on a Greyhound bus to go check it out.

After a three-hour ride staring out at roadways lined with orange trees and distant snowcapped mountains, the small town of Palm Springs, by comparison, looked bleak in the late afternoon sun, not anywhere near as beautiful as I'd read about in magazines.

As soon as I checked into the Palm Springs Hotel, I threw my suitcase into the small room and headed down to the lobby's empty bar, noticing only one other person sitting alone.

A few minutes later, the other customer, a man in his twenties with heavy-lidded brown eyes and short-cropped hair wearing an open-necked polo shirt and khaki pants, waved and introduced himself as Bob. Since we were the only two people here, he wondered if I'd like to talk for a while. We began to chat, he asked questions about my life, why I was there, and where I was staying, but offered little information about himself. As we talked, he mentioned it was getting late and that he had to return to the newly opened Howard Manor Hotel (where he was staying) to freshen up before dinner, but if I didn't have dinner plans, I could join him.

An hour later, he came back in a Chevy convertible with the top down, and we drove to the famous CHI CHI restaurant/nightclub. The maître d' recognized Bob, calling him by name, and asked him to wait a few minutes at the bar. We ordered a couple of drinks and Bob handed the bartender a five-dollar tip when he paid the bill. The two drinks were much less, and I thought the tip was extravagant, but it was his money, not mine.

After dinner and watching the show with the flamboyant performer Arthur Blake, we took a drive through the empty desert, reveling in the warm air and millions of stars in the sky, and then to his hotel where I spent the night.

The following morning, he suggested rather than staying in my hotel that I come to stay with him instead. We both agreed it was silly to pay for an empty room once it was obvious we'd be spending more than one night together. Without hesitation, I checked out of my place and moved into his large poolside suite.

Pink oleanders surrounded the hotel and pool boys brought us drinks and lunch as we lounged beside the large gleaming pool. Each day at two in the afternoon, as I lay by the pool, Bob walked into the suite to make what he said was a business telephone call, which I thought nothing about at the time.

Wherever we went for dinner he seemed to be recognized by the maître d' and always left the barman the same five-dollar tip (the equivalent of about sixty dollars today) which I increasingly found strange.

After staying with him for five days, he mentioned he had a private plane at the Palm Springs airport and was going to go to Mexico City to meet his friend, the ex-New York mayor William O'Dwyer and his girlfriend. Bob asked me if I wanted to come along. I said I'd love to go but first had to return to Los Angeles and inform my employer and roommate about my plans.

When I arrived in LA, my roommate handed me a special delivery letter from the Military Induction Center instructing me to report a few weeks later. I immediately telephoned Bob at the hotel but was told he had checked out shortly after I left. I was completely mystified by his actions, but I'd be lying if I didn't say I wasn't also a bit intrigued and seduced by his air of mystery.

As soon as I got my final induction notice, I wrote to a couple of friends stationed at the Fort Ord Army base in Northern California telling them to expect me shortly. Boy, was I wrong.

At the Induction Center in downtown LA, standing in a circle with thirty naked fellow inductees, a sergeant announced that one out of fifteen of us would be put into the Marine Corps and sent for training at MCRD in San Diego. I was number fifteen. When they called my number, my knees buckled. Later, when I called my parents to inform them of the change from the Army to the Marines, my mother dropped the phone.

Seated next to me on the bus taking us to boot camp was an inductee who had been born in Finland and joined to obtain his United States citizenship. We began chatting and somehow bonded, becoming buddies, equally nervous about our unknown future.

An accompanying drill sergeant instructor walked up and down the aisle of the bus screaming profanities at us newbies and barking that we civilians were going to be taught to be Killer Marines, so we had better shape up fast.

At that, my new buddy and I sat straight up for the rest of the trip and didn't utter a word but stayed deep in our minds. I thought if this is a game, whatever it might be, I am going to play it.

Boot camp was tough training and after two weeks I figured out how to play the game, swearing and strutting in my fatigues just like the macho guys. A drill instructor said he'd read my folder and seeing I was a pianist asked me to give him a private performance one afternoon. There was a piano in a Quonset hut and he sat alone in the empty room listening to me play.

Early one morning, our battalion was standing Dress Right Dress, our heads turned to the right and our left hands poised on our left hips. As he inspected each one of us, Captain Mercer came up behind me and whispered, "You look like you should be wearing furs and draped in jewels." I tried not to laugh and stared straight ahead, knowing it was only my Finnish buddy who'd heard. Afterward, he and I named him Captain "Mabel Mercer" (after the New York jazz singer).

How I managed to maintain some level of competency in an extremely difficult six weeks was amazing, but I passed my tests and graduated as Private First Class.

My assignment to the 3rd Marine Division was at Camp Pendleton in San Onofre, California, just a few miles south of Laguna Beach, a small town that happened to have two gay bars at the time. The Boom Boom Room was frequented by officers and Las Ondas (also known as Camille's) was for us enlisted men. Las Ondas' best feature was a back door that opened directly to the beach where we could run and hide in the darkness when the Shore Patrol entered the front door looking to arrest us for being there, even though we were out of uniform.

My Pendleton job assignment was a clerk in the Supply Department where I handed out rifles and fatigue uniforms. It was like the work I'd done in civilian life with the same 9 a.m. to 5 p.m. hours Monday through Friday, with occasional additional training in firearms and tactics.

Often at 5 a.m., we were required to be at the Supply Store and hand out rifles to barely trained Marines who were to be airlifted to Korea. This was toward the end of the "conflict" and, unbeknownst to them, they were soon to be slaughtered in the infamous Battle of Bunker Hill. It was then that I began to fervently pray that I wouldn't be sent to Korea.

On Friday mornings during roll call, our battalion would be standing at attention and frequently there'd be calls down the line from someone asking, "Hey, you guys going up to that Hollywood producer George Cukor's for the weekend? Lots of beer and chow." I'd always yell back that I had other plans because although it was tempting, I knew not only beer but also sex was going to be provided to my buddies and they would have discovered I was gay because I might have liked the sex a little too much. My buddy Marines were all supposedly straight, but that didn't stop them from receiving fellatio. They somehow justified that as okay and "not gay."

Each morning on a work break I'd grab a coffee at the PX, and on one of those mornings, there was a new guy behind the counter. He was tall, tan, blond, and very good-looking. The only thing missing was the white line of sunscreen on his nose; I recognized him from our volleyball games on Will Rogers State Beach in Santa Monica, from before we were inducted into the Marine Corps.

After reintroducing myself, we decided to meet that evening for a drink at Las Ondas in Laguna. His name was Al, from Pasadena, and he too had been drafted into the Marines, having recently arrived at Pendleton.

Al and I fell in lust. I suppose it was more out of the convenience of being stationed together than anything else because we shared few mutual interests. But that didn't stop us. We took whatever private weekend evenings we had to check into a cheap motel in Laguna or lie on the beach in nearby Dana Point.

On one of those beach nights, we noticed a strange-looking object that seemed to hover above the water. It had blue lights that flickered on and off, and after a few minutes, it suddenly whisked away. We were certain it wasn't the moon because we saw that shining in another direction. Later that week, it was reported the object had been seen up and down the West Coast by multiple witnesses, and it was presumed to be a flying saucer. We knew we couldn't tell anyone what we'd seen because there would have been too many questions as to how, where, and why—and our cover would have been blown.

Soon, however, our secret liaisons became known to others, because we were both summoned into the Colonel's office and told he had damning information about our Laguna weekends together. Our names had been given to him by a disgruntled gay sailor attached to the base who had broken up with his Marine Corps boyfriend. He was offered a sort of plea deal if he offered up the names of other gay people. Al and I were taken into separate rooms and drilled about our activities. I tried denying all the allegations, but they showed me evidence to the contrary, including written reports naming the motel we'd stayed at and detailing our actions, saying if I admitted it and gave them other names I would be quietly discharged, and they wouldn't inform our parents we were homos. I admitted nothing and didn't offer any names, but many people did, and it quickly snowballed. Before long, people were turning in chaplains, nurses, and naval attachments stationed with us. In all, over 120 people were kicked out of Camp Pendleton.

Without lawyers to defend us, we were arrested and put into five-by-eight-foot cells in the brig with other Marines and Navy personnel. Each cell had a mattress on the floor and a toilet and nothing else. We were only taken out to exercise, shower, or be led in marching ranks to the Mess Hall, where on each of the long tables was a sign that read WOMEN MARINES, which was intended for us.

Every day in the cell I sang the Dinah Washington song "What a Difference a Day Makes." The song lifted my spirits and told me I would soon be out of there.

When I was released after a couple of weeks or so, they sent me back to the same tent I'd shared with five other buddies before my arrest. All of them hugged me except one, saying we were Marine buddies and that no matter what had happened they would always stand by me.

Confined to the base for another month while awaiting discharge, I had little to do because most of the other Marines were on maneuvers in barges off the beach in San Onofre. While awaiting papers to go on leave, a supposedly heterosexual buddy came to my tent offering a massage, which surprisingly ended with a mutual sexual experience. I never thought about doing anything sexual on base but at that point, I thought what the hell, I knew I was leaving soon anyway.

When the day of our discharge arrived, those of us who were to be discharged for being gay were ordered to wear our dress uniforms and put on our full battle ribbons. The prized ribbons, worn on the left side of the chest, commemorated where our division had fought worldwide.

We were then marched onto the parade field, where other battalions were watching. The captain commanded us to stand at attention. Then the drums rolled loudly and a general strode up. Stopping in front of us, he proceeded to violently rip the battle ribbons off our Marine uniforms one by one until he got to the end of the line. It felt as though my heart had been torn from my body. I tried not to cry while I rigidly stood there. All I could think was, *Marines don't cry.*

Upon my release, I was given an Undesirable Discharge, but I hid it from nearly everyone. I told my parents that I'd hurt my back during maneuvers and been released on medical grounds, and they never questioned me.

Before I'd entered the Marine Corps, I was floating around six feet off the ground having a good time, but the moment I got on that bus going to boot camp I felt a change happening. Ultimately, the good and bad experiences of being groomed as a killer Marine, and then being thrown out, grounded me. I learned to protect myself in most situations, to appreciate the camaraderie of friends, to swear like a toughie, and to slowly create the person I am today.

During the 1980s I read in the *LA Times* obituaries that my Marine Corps paramour Al had died. As I read the article, I could still remember his sunburnt nose and the golden hair on his muscular legs. It was then I finally cried.

As soon as I was out of the Marine Corps, I felt a little disconnected from the life around me. I knew I wanted to remain in the Los Angeles area and searching the ads in the Santa Monica and Westwood Village newspapers, I found a Westwood apartment to share with two guys from Tennessee. Michael, a dancer at MGM, and Ken, a salesman at Desmond's, a luxury men's store. Ken told me there was an opening at his store in Men's Furnishings and encouraged me to apply. Shortly thereafter, I began to work there.

It was one of those hot July days, and the store was empty of customers. Business had been dead that day and we salesmen in the Men's Furnishings department were bored. We were on a rotating system, and it was my turn to be "up" to help the next customer. While waiting near the back entrance, I saw a long black limousine pull into the parking lot behind the store. Silhouetted against the sun-washed white wall, the black car gleamed and looked quite impressive. The door opened and an older man, supported by a white cane and dressed in white pants and a bright-colored Madras sport jacket, which shimmered in the hot July sun, emerged from the vehicle. This was to be my customer.

When the gentleman entered the store, I approached him and asked if I might be of assistance.

"Yes," he said. "I want to buy a dozen pairs of silk undershorts."

I immediately started doing the math in my head, adding up the 7% commission on a dozen pairs at $7.50 each. I explained we only had two pairs of shorts in stock but could special order more for him. He agreed and asked that I measure his waist to be certain of the size. He walked to a three-way mirror and proceeded to unbutton his pants while telling me he was certain his waist was size 32. As I watched him slowly unbutton his pants, the thought occurred to me that this little old man might have more on his mind than just getting me to measure his waist, but I ignored the thought and did my best to proceed as professionally as possible. After measuring, I told him the tape size showed a 34 and not a 32. He insisted vehemently it was impossible to be a size 34, and then conceded that perhaps he had gained some weight after all as he struggled to rebutton his pants.

I explained that the shorts would be ordered, but they would have to be paid for in advance, asking if it would be cash or charge. (In 1953, a "charge" was a store account. Credit cards did not exist.) He said it was a charge and then I asked him for his information, starting with his name.

I began to write as he spelled out his name, "C-O-L-E, P-O-R-" and at that, I did a double take and wrote the rest of his name and his phone number with a shaky hand before telling him the order would arrive in one week. He thanked me and left the store—leaving me with my mouth hanging open.

Just the week before, a friend who was a frequent guest of Porter had told me a story about attending pool parties at Porter's place on Rockingham Road in Brentwood. Each Sunday afternoon during the summer, he had his houseman invite twelve good-looking young men to lunch and swim in his large pool. These same twelve men, on subsequent Sundays, were to bring other equally handsome men.

While the men were swimming and lying by the pool, Porter would arrive, introduce himself to each one, and then disappear, only to be seen later standing in his upstairs window watching the men swim. I'd heard of this when Porter ordered the silk shorts and fantasized that he might invite me when he returned to pick up the package.

A week later, I telephoned the Porter residence to let them know his order had arrived. The following day, the same sleek black limousine arrived in the parking lot, but to my disappointment, it was the houseman, not Porter, who exited the limo and came in to pick up the order.

Later, when I told my friend of my dashed fantasy, he explained I was not "hot" enough to be invited anyway. I was by no means unattractive and had no trouble finding guys who were interested in me, but I guess I certainly was not the desired "Hollywood beauty". Apparently, at the end of that summer, the original twelve men who had been guests of Porter were given a Tiffany key ring inscribed with the date and Porter's signature. Of course, not having been invited to those afternoons I didn't get one and I'd have to wait a while longer before I'd be invited to any exciting Hollywood parties.

Four months after I was discharged from the Marine Corps, I took a long weekend off work and went back to Palm Springs for some much-needed relaxation. On my first evening, I stopped at the CHI CHI for a drink. The bartender, surprised to see me, said, "Do you know the FBI has been looking all over the place for you? Seems your friend Bob robbed a Brinks truck in Boston, and they just recently had some leads to his whereabouts."

Shock gripped me. In an instant, everything came into crystal-clear focus. All the extravagant tips, the mysterious afternoon phone calls, and the plane to Mexico suddenly made perfect sense. Like the rest of the country, I had read about the Great Brinks Robbery in

Boston the year before. Today's equivalent of about 33 million dollars had been stolen, making it the biggest theft in US history at the time, and here I had been intimate with one of the robbers. No wonder he fled to Mexico with the FBI on his trail.

I discovered that "Bob" was Joseph O'Keefe, who would eventually testify against his accomplices. I'll never know whether his intended meeting with the former mayor of New York was true, but I do know it was certainly a memorable first trip to Palm Springs.

As it turned out, my new roommates were party boys and I started partying along with them, which was fun as it was happening but often resulted in being badly hungover the morning after. I began arriving to work later and later each day. After being admonished numerous times by my department boss, the store manager finally called me into his office one morning and said he felt I wasn't keen on working there and that it was probably best for us to part ways. I agreed and was mercifully fired, which enabled me to collect unemployment insurance.

With the first real free time I'd had since being in the Service, I found myself going to Crystal Beach in Ocean Park nearly every day. The beach was always crowded with gay men lying in the sun or coming in and out of the bathhouse along the boardwalk, where there were a couple of bars and a hamburger stand as well.

One of those bars was The Tropical Village, owned by the affable George Ball who, always smiling, welcomed a clientele of gay men, lesbians, and many Hollywood celebrities such as Rita Hayworth, Vivien Leigh, Lawrence Olivier, Ali Khan, and others. A small lesbian band played music to accompany the occasional dancers on the minuscule dance floor. It was at this bar that I would meet a person who would become a fascinating part of my life.

One evening, I walked into the crowded bar and after being

greeted by George, was excitedly told, "A real princess is coming. Princess Radziwill is going to be arriving any minute now." Shortly thereafter, a beautiful, statuesque blonde wearing a bright red Dior coat and flashing a gorgeous smile walked in and was quickly surrounded by admirers. We were introduced and somewhere in the conversation, she was told I had lived in New York. This seemed to spike her interest because she had also lived in New York. She began asking me questions about where I was from, what was I doing in California, and so on. Then she suggested we sit down and have a drink together, which led to her telling me she was living in Malibu, had recently been robbed of her jewelry, and was afraid of living alone. Then with seeming innocence, before we'd even finished our second drink, she asked out of the blue if I would like to live with her.

"Lois," I said, "as generous as that offer is, I simply don't think it would be possible because I'm afraid I don't currently have a car or steady work."

I feared she might have thought less of me since I had just admitted to being unemployed and carless, but she didn't bat an eye, and we continued chatting for most of the evening.

Lois and I enjoyed one another's company on subsequent evenings, laughing and drinking and exchanging stories about New York and her European escapades, or joking about our families and friends who were stuck in the Midwest. It turns out that she was born in North Dakota, and I was of course from Minnesota, so that cemented our fast friendship.

Lois had a Grace Kelly aura about her but lacked Grace's fine facial features. At nearly six feet tall, what Lois didn't lack was charisma and sex appeal. Born Lois Olson, she grew up in Bismarck, the daughter of poor Norwegian-American parents. Lois ran off at seventeen to marry a sailor, divorced him after a short while and moved to New York City to join her sister, who was a showgirl at the fabled Copacabana nightclub.

Paraphrasing a Bette Davis line from the film *Now, Voyager*, Lois liked to say, "If you reach for the stars, you're sure to get the moon." In her case it was true—at least in the beginning.

It was in New York in 1949 when Lois's life changed dramatically. She was waiting for a stoplight to change at the corner of 57th Street and Fifth Avenue when a handsome, well-dressed European gentleman twenty years her senior commented to his friend that the girl standing next to them was the most attractive woman he'd seen in New York. Overhearing the conversation, Lois thanked the tall stranger and jokingly said that he was the handsomest man she'd seen in that city. After a brief conversation, he invited her to dinner, beginning a long, intimate, and rocky relationship. The man was Alex Berglas, a wealthy French textile manufacturer.

Over the next few weeks, Alex began to lavish Lois with gifts of jewelry and clothes. Charmed by her naivete yet chagrined by her lack of social acumen, he convinced her to return with him to Colmar, France, where she could learn French and German, and the social graces. In retrospect, Berglas might have been creating a French version of George Bernard Shaw's Pygmalion. What emerged from this transformation was a poised, charming "great beauty" adept in language, makeup, and wardrobe. When their relationship finally soured over Lois's bohemian lifestyle, she married Berglas's closest friend, the seventy-year-old Prince Stanislaw Radziwill, heir to the defunct Polish throne. Soon after, the marriage fell apart.

Lois realized it was Alex Berglas she really loved after all. She went back to him; then Berglas came home from a business trip to find his Eliza Doolittle in bed with another woman. In a rage, he cut off Lois's beautiful blonde hair, triggering a nervous breakdown and a recuperation at the famed Bircher-Benner sanatorium in Switzerland.

Yes, I'd heard and read all sorts of bizarre rumors about her marriage, her pending divorce, and her free-spirited lifestyle. Most of the rumors proved to be true. So after her European life, Lois was in California to be near her family, who had since moved to Venice, and to recuperate from her ordeal with Alex.

Not long after we met, she told me she had moved out of the Malibu house and rented a small place on Mesa Drive in Santa Monica Canyon. She asked me once again to move in with her, this time telling me I had no good excuses.

I was still unemployed and without a car, so in my mind, I had every excuse not to be living with a literal princess. She wouldn't take no for an answer, though, and by the following weekend, I had moved in with her.

Our friendship blossomed and I became a confidant, hearing her stories of life in Europe, problems with her estranged husband Prince Radziwill, and the fascinating tale of a small-town American girl who became a princess.

While driving back to Santa Monica from a dinner in Beverly Hills one evening, Lois casually mentioned that numerous royal European friends of hers were arriving for the summer and, because of their anti-Semitic views, would I mind changing my name from Cohen (my then surname) to a more anglicized name. A bit drunk and remembering how my dad had changed his name to get a job, I agreed, but with one proviso: I would keep my initials, L. C. Just then, a Chrysler car passed, and we both screamed, "That's it!" And from that moment on, I became Larry Chrysler.

When my birthday rolled around, Lois invited a group of her friends to celebrate by first going to a performance at the Hollywood Bowl and then to a posh La Cienega restaurant for dinner afterward. She busied herself that day going to the bank to get her jewels out of the vault and then to the hairdresser to have her hair and makeup done. That evening—she in her navy-blue shantung silk Dior suit, pearls, and jewelry, and I in my blue blazer—we shared a cocktail before leaving the Mesa Drive house, ready for a fabulous night on the town. Our spirits were both high, and I felt like a million dollars. Then, just as we were preparing to leave the house, the doorbell rang, and a messenger delivered to me a gift of a beautiful bouquet of red roses from Princess Zina Rachevsky, a Russian lesbian and dear friend of Lois.

There were eight of us in two adjoining boxes at the Bowl and after the performance, we caravanned to the restaurant. After dinner, Lois invited everyone to come by the house for a nightcap. Zina arrived first and, upon entering, said she had to go to the restroom where we heard a scream. Zina angrily stormed out and slammed the door behind her, because she'd discovered her gift of roses was sitting in the toilet bowl. Earlier, in the rush to leave the house and with no time to put the flowers in a vase, I had placed them in the toilet so they would at least have water until we got home. But of course, then I'd forgotten once we'd been out drinking all night. Zina didn't speak to me for two weeks after that.

At two one morning, leaving the Tropical Village bar, Lois suggested her girlfriend Betty Doss (a former Miss New Orleans) and I drive to San Francisco. With no money in my pocket, Lois in her magnificent red Dior coat wearing nothing underneath, and Betty stoned on marijuana, we all climbed into Lois's Cadillac, and off we went up the Pacific Coast Highway. I fell asleep in the back seat and awakened to realize Lois was driving about twenty miles per hour and was also very stoned. I told her to drive faster, and she replied, "I am flying honey . . . *flying.*"

When we finally arrived, I telephoned a friend of mine, asking to stay and to borrow some money. Lois and Betty stayed with a friend of theirs. I didn't see them again during my stay and after a few days, I flew back to Los Angeles alone.

That episode did it for me and I decided this kind of life was too much. I moved out of the Mesa house and rented a small apartment.

We had a heated phone call after the San Francisco trip and a few arguments as I was moving my things out, but we both knew it was for the best. I couldn't keep living like that, and she wasn't about to change.

About six months later, I ran into her at the Tropical Village where we'd first met, and she told me of divorcing the prince and her off-and-on-again affair with the French textile magnate Alex Berglas. Letting bygones be bygones, we chatted for a long while, and by the end of the month, she'd convinced me to move in with her again.

Lois had moved to Nichols Canyon in the time since we'd last lived together, renting an airy but isolated house up a dirt road on a promontory with a marvelous view of the city. The neighbors across the road were Lena Horne and her pianist husband Lennie Hayton. Walking late at night along the deserted road, I'd often hear piano music coming from the windows of the Horne/Hayton house, but I never heard any singing.

Day and night, the Princess surrounded herself with hangers-on, primarily expensive call girls and boys with their celebrity johns, all of whom did heavy drugs. I wasn't interested in the drugs but was fascinated by the cast of characters coming in and out of the house.

Other than getting high—and getting into frequent arguments

with Betty, who had also moved in by this point—Lois's main focus was on the possibility of rejoining Alex. One day, she nervously awaited an important telegram from him affirming the decision for her to return to him in Europe. After dinner that evening, she took off her jewels, stashed most of them in small flowerpots under the kitchen sink, and then, looking closely at a beautiful long strand of white pearls, told me if they were not worn, they would turn yellowish, and would I please wear them during the night while I slept.

That night, I was wearing the black silk pajamas that had been given to me as a Christmas gift from actor George Raft, Betty's john, and laughing, we decided the pearls were a perfect accessory. In the middle of the night, the doorbell rang. My bedroom was closest, and I opened the front door to see the shocked face of a Western Union messenger delivering the long-awaited telegram from Europe. I had forgotten I was wearing the pearls.

Alex had started sending Western Union checks to sustain Lois's now meager lifestyle, which had started with her and some of her friends smoking marijuana and slowly progressing to harder drugs and more frequent drama. First came something called goofballs, which they often drank with alcohol. Then it was cocaine, and finally, heroin. This was the beginning of the end of my relationship with the princess.

Shaun was a good-looking gay man my age who was always hanging around the house and worked nights as a high-priced call boy. He once asked me if I would have sex with him in front of a well-known Hollywood actor, saying we'd be paid hundreds of dollars each. As tempting as it might have been for others, I refused, and that was when I decided for the second time I'd had enough of the so-called high life and moved out.

After that, I would see Lois occasionally at a party, and our relationship remained as amiable as it could be given the circumstances. But my life had changed, and she seemed to be even more immersed in drugs, so I backed away and decided privately not to continue the friendship.

My California adventure wasn't exactly what I'd call off to a smashing start. There had been an Undesirable Discharge from the Marines, partying roommates, a close call with a conman in the desert, and a bona fide princess who, as charming and glamorous and generous as she'd once been, ultimately ripped through my life like a tornado. All of this might have left me disillusioned to the point of hopping on the first train back East if it hadn't been for the exquisite timing of a gentleman who would forever change my life.

1953. Sandy and I in costume for a party hosted
by Baron Herbert Hischmoeller.
From the author's collection.

SIX

Love Can Be A Moment's Madness

It was a month before my twenty-second birthday when my friend Johnny Johnson offered to throw me a birthday party. One day he called and said I should come by his Westwood Village apartment after my nighttime art classes at the Chouinard Art Institute to discuss the guest list, and that there was someone he wanted me to meet. After class, not having a car and anxious to know who this person could be, I stuck out my thumb and hitchhiked to Westwood Village. Back then, hitchhiking was commonplace; we never thought twice about doing it when necessary.

When I arrived at Johnny's spare midcentury apartment, he led me into the living room where I saw an older man sitting on a large floor cushion. He stayed seated when Johnny introduced us, and as I walked closer to him, I noticed his eyes and slicked-back hair were deep ebony. He wore a tight white Lacoste polo shirt, faded blue Levi's, white sweat socks, and scuffed brown loafers. I was immediately taken by his good looks and classic style, but his decision not to stand up to greet me was unnerving and made me think he might be a little arrogant.

"Frank Tack," he said, holding out his hand for me to shake. "Yes, Tack," he added, "as in thumb tack."

Little did I know this would be the man who would become one of the most important people in my life.

The conversation that evening was mainly about my upcoming birthday party, and Frank let it be known he was sorry he couldn't attend as he had other plans that weekend. It had been a nice night, and I'd grown fond of Frank, but I couldn't tell if it was mutual or not since I was also trying to focus on planning the party. I did worry that I might not get another chance to see him, but luckily, when he found out I didn't have a car as we were leaving, he graciously offered to drive me to my nearby Veteran Avenue apartment.

As he drove his old beat-up '48 Oldsmobile convertible, I kept glancing at him out of the corner of my eye, thinking how good-looking he was and wondering if what I was feeling was reciprocal. When we arrived at my apartment and before getting out of the car, I managed to ask him if we might meet again. He smiled rather perfunctorily and said it wouldn't be possible because he was very busy, and the weekend of my party he was going with a lady friend to the opening of a show in Las Vegas. It seemed that his entire upcoming month was booked solid. We shook hands, said the obligatory "Nice having met you," and he drove off. I walked up to my apartment feeling a bit sad after his cool rejection.

Sometimes, however, fate has a way of toying with you, and what you first thought to be a fact turns out to be something else entirely. A few months later, a friend took me to a party in the Hollywood Hills. Upon entering the house, I immediately saw Frank Tack. I couldn't believe it, so after a drink or two, I approached him and asked if he remembered me. He smiled and said what I later learned was a notorious pickup line of his: "You never call." I replied that I didn't have his telephone number, to which he took a small leather case out of his navy blazer pocket and, with a tiny gold pen, wrote his name and number on a piece of cream-colored notepaper. The case was emblazoned with the name Mark Cross, an expensive New York leather goods store, and seeing that I thought, *Hmmm, good taste too!* He was then whisked away by a friend whom I later learned he had been dating. We never spoke again that evening, but now and then I would steal a glance at him and sometimes catch him looking at me, too. Still, I assumed that since he was with someone else and he'd blown me off the first time, I didn't stand much of a chance.

After waiting a couple of weeks so I didn't seem too anxious, I called and invited him to a movie and dinner the following Saturday night. To my surprise, he readily accepted the invitation. I was thrilled. And nervous! The night of our first date, he picked me up at my apartment, and we went to a movie theater on Pico Boulevard in West Los Angeles where we sat in the crowded balcony. After the film, we went for spaghetti across the street at Maria's Italian Restaurant.

Over dinner, we discovered we had much in common: we were both pianists and loved classical music as well as jazz, we shared a mutual interest in languages (I had learned German and he spoke German and French), and he had lived in a penthouse apartment at 405 East 54th Street—the same apartment, coincidentally, that I had visited many times when I lived in New York and it had been occupied by my friend, the jeweler David Webb.

In retrospect, Frank was the type of man who would never in his life have gone to a movie theater or sat in the balcony on a Saturday night. And yet he did that night, and happily went along with the entire experience.

We began dating, going out to restaurants and parties where he introduced me to his friends. One told me Frank said he was dating a hot ex-Marine, which I found hysterically funny. Some of his close friends were skeptical of our budding relationship due to our twenty-year age difference, assuming I might be a gold-digger.

Frank mentioned a friend who had a boyfriend who needed a roommate, and I began to share an elegant Brentwood flat with Dane Akers, a window designer at Bullock's Westwood department store, where I happened to be working in Men's Furnishings. At the same time I was dating Frank, Dane was dating Frank's equally older friend, the very rich antique dealer Jimmy Pendleton.

Dane and I were like the proverbial "Little Girls from Little Rock," the song from the musical *Gentlemen Prefer Blondes*. The only difference was we were two young men dating older men and gleefully comparing notes from the previous night's escapades.

SEVEN

High Society

Our dates became more frequent, although we weren't exclusive to one another. When Frank felt comfortable enough with me, we socialized more with his friends. His closest was Virginia Burrows, a contemporary of his living in an apartment in the elegant Chateau Marmont hotel.

Virginia was a tall, imposing woman of a "certain age," and we referred to her as Madame Pompadour; her hair was always piled high and perfectly tinted auburn, the epitome of chic. Her magnificent jewelry had been designed personally for her by Louis Arpels of Paris' Place Vendome jewelers Van Cleef & Arpels. Among her collection was a bracelet of Cabochon emeralds the size of eggs, a magnificent deep blue emerald-cut sapphire and gold ring she only wore to lunch, a butterfly brooch with a hundred and twenty moveable tiny diamonds (which she couldn't afford to insure so she had it sewn into whatever dress she would wear that evening), and many other equally important pieces.

Each evening between five and seven o'clock she hosted a salon in her Chateau Marmont apartment, mixing high society and the artistic, which was always a scintillating and interesting group that made for the best conversation. As a "Mother Confessor" figure who was known for doling out sage advice, she welcomed the opportunity to speak privately with her friends if one of us had personal problems. I found myself on multiple occasions pouring my heart out to her about the issues I'd started having with Frank, only for her to wave her magic wand and lift my spirits just in time for her guests to start arriving. Her warmth and graciousness always made things seem better.

With cocktails, she provided a simple plate with cherry tomatoes and next to it, a plate of half salt and half pepper. Nothing else. No expensive hors d'oeuvres. Nothing but that, drinks, and good conversation.

The famous Hollywood couturier Howard Greer gifted her with dresses from his new collections because despite all evidence to the contrary, "Virg" didn't have much money. Each Wednesday, she drove a Cadillac convertible, she named Miss Beige, west on Sunset Boulevard to the John Wolfe-designed Regency-style house across the street from the Beverly Hills Hotel. There, she'd pick up her friend Dorothy "Dodo" Pendleton, an equally elegant woman always dressed by the French designer Balmain and married to openly gay (among us) Jimmy Pendleton. The "girls" would then drive to the exclusive Romanov's restaurant in Beverly Hills for their weekly luncheon. They were the original Ladies Who Lunch.

Around that time, Bobby Short, a cabaret singer/pianist, was performing regularly at the Cafe Gala on the Sunset Strip. His first recording came out that year, and I listened to it over and over, amazed at how he sang the lyrics to the song and played a counterpoint jazz accompaniment. On Saturday mornings there was a radio show that would play new singing artists' recordings and invite famous musicians to critique them without being told the name of the singer. A popular vocal group, The Four Freshmen, were guest judges, and after hearing Bobby's first recording, they were asked their opinions. Among the compliments, one said, "I don't know who she is, but I love her voice." At the time, Bobby's voice and diction mirrored his singing heroine, Mabel Mercer.

A year after the celebration he'd missed out on when we'd first met, Frank made up for it by offering to throw me a birthday party. He said that Bobby would be one of the guests and that I could have Bobby autograph the jacket of his recording. Frank had neglected to invite any of my actual friends, but the people he did invite were all talented well-known singers and musicians like Broadway stars Mary McCarty and Ella Logan, pianist Billy Roy, MGM pianist Roger Eden, and others.

When I ended up feeling uncomfortable at my party because I didn't know any of the guests, Bobby came over and sat next to me on the sofa, making a special effort to engage me in conversation. I later discovered this was another talent of his: making people feel comfortable either with his music or chatting. What a gift. That evening was the first of what was to be a fifty-year friendship.

Another fascinating friend of Frank's was Lloyd Pantages, heir to a movie theater chain and an old landowning family in California. Lloyd was perpetually leather-tanned, and he hosted what was to be my first "Hollywood" cocktail party in his apartment at the art deco Sunset Towers. Upon arriving, the guests were quickly introduced to us. I was so nervous, the only names I caught were one of the sons of Franklin D. Roosevelt, the heiress Doris Duke with her piano-playing lover, and Lloyd's niece Erin, who was a pretty young girl.

During cocktails, I was sitting on the sofa mainly conversing with Erin when a buffet dinner was announced. The simple dinner was set up on a table in front of a large bay window overlooking Los Angeles, and the guests quickly gathered around, filling their plates with creamed chicken and vegetables. Ignored by Frank and not knowing how to go about serving myself, I guess I looked as bewildered as I felt because Ms. Duke walked up to me, leaned over, and smilingly offered to bring me my dinner of creamed chicken. I simply didn't know the rituals and the pomp of this society. I was nervous and afraid I'd spill something or use a serving utensil in the wrong way.

The following morning, I called my mother, eager to tell her about meeting Doris Duke. Her response? "What the hell were *you* doing with Doris Duke?"

As the parties I was attending got more and more glamorous, my work life was getting more and more pathetic. I couldn't hold down a job to save my life, and I found myself uninterested in anything that didn't challenge or stimulate me. I wanted to do something great and knew that I could, but the reality of where I was compared to the people at those parties seemed like such a monumental distance. I often felt inadequate before I came into my own professional life, hoping people didn't ask me detailed questions about what I did for work.

Fired from Bullock's for giving an employee discount to a friend, I was without a job again. Because I'd been spending more time with Frank, I decided to find a job and apartment closer to his Beverly Hills house. Very soon, a couple of friends my age offered to share their two-story apartment on Flores Avenue in West Hollywood, and I quickly found a bank teller job at the Ahmanson Bank, which allowed me to stay at my new apartment during the week and at Frank's house on weekends.

One of Frank's friends was a vice president at the Ahmanson Bank in Beverly Hills, and he's the one who hired me to work as a teller. But working a nine-to-five job behind a cage dealing with money was so boring, that I quit after a month. The only thing I recall about the work was that my hands were always dirty from handling the cash. I'd heard that if I'd stayed through Christmas, I would be invited to Mr. Ahmanson's Hancock Park house where he would play his huge pipe organ for the employees, but that was not enough to keep me there, so I politely told the man who'd hired me only a month ago that I was moving on and immediately started searching for something more stimulating.

I tried job after job to no avail, lasting less time and having increasingly less enthusiasm at each new place. At one point, an employment agency found a job for me as a file clerk at an insurance company, but it was so mind-numbing I don't even recall how long I worked there, the name of the company, or the exact location.

Then, when I heard that a new Beverly Hills store, Robinson's, had just opened, I applied for a position in the Men's Furnishings department and soon got hired. This lifted my spirits and gave me some hope because it was closer to my dreams and skill set. I was required to attend three days of orientation before being allowed on the selling floor. Four of us prospective salespersons sat in a small, bare-bones room near the employee entrance learning to use the cash register, write sales invoices, and understand the philosophy of the exclusive department store. The woman who taught us how a sales invoice should be written repeated over and over, "Tear the tissue." Sitting there bored out of my mind, I kept hearing her say, "Care to kiss you."

After three days of orientation, I arrived early on my first day on the sales floor wanting to become familiar with the merchandise I was going to sell. Promptly at 10 a.m. when the doors opened, I greeted my first customer—a tall, very tan, blonde lady who asked in a distinct New-Yorkaise accent if we had any "Bahn Sower" pajamas. "They are very expensive," she said.

"Excuse me. You must mean Bon Soir silk pajamas," I haughtily said, saying the name in my fake French accent.

"Oh yeah, that must be them," she said.

After selling her a pair of pajamas, I thought, "If this is the kind of customer who shops in this store I don't want to work here." So, at the end of the day, I left without telling anyone.

Finally, after a long series of terrible jobs came the icing on the cake. Or, in this case, the coffee in the cup. I'd been hired to work behind the counter of a short-order cafe in Westwood, which I thought would be an easy job. The first (and last) morning on the job, I arrived spiffed up in my uniform, a white apron, T-shirt, khakis, and white buck leather shoes. When lunchtime hit, the place suddenly filled with customers yelling requests.

"Coffee!"

"Sandwiches!"

"Desserts!"

I was overwhelmed, and this time, I thanked the nice boss and left that same afternoon with coffee splattered on my new white shoes. If nothing else, at least I'd improved on my exit strategy.

After thinking long and hard about my job woes, I realized my irresponsible behavior had to stop. But how? What was the problem? It was then I fully realized I was going to become a dress designer come hell or high water. The problem was that I wasn't doing what I was meant to do. I wasn't going after what I truly wanted, and I wasn't living my passion. How was I going to do it? I had no idea, but somehow, some way, I knew I would think of something. I knew my angels hadn't brought me this far to let me squander away my life.

EIGHT

The Beginning Of Love

Over the next few months, my relationship with Frank continued to develop and become serious. One sunny Sunday afternoon, we were driving home from the beach in his Olds with the top down and the radio blaring Ella Fitzgerald singing, "This is the end of a beautiful friendship and the beginning of love." Hearing those lyrics that day made me realize, right then and there, that I had fallen in love with him. I took his hand and held it as he drove home, feeling like we were now, at last, a couple.

A few months after that day, Frank suggested we spend the New Year's holiday weekend in Palm Springs, so we drove down and found a cute hotel bungalow to stay in. On New Year's Eve, we had a great time celebrating at the CHI CHI watching gay performer Arthur Blake's antics. Of course, we woke early the next morning with terrible hangovers. Frank, who was an accomplished horseman (having ridden at the prestigious Rolling Rock Club in Pennsylvania) said the fresh desert air would be good for us if we went horseback riding. I, who'd only ridden before with a group walking on a trail, for some reason thought this sounded like a great idea and that it would be an adventure.

We drove to the Smoke Tree Ranch and rented two big, beautiful horses. Frank quickly climbed onto the saddle of his horse, jauntily riding out of the stable and then patiently waiting as I awkwardly mounted mine. Very slowly, we trotted out into the barren desert with the early morning sunshine casting its golden glow on us. Despite our hangovers, I remember thinking we looked like a perfect desert cowboy couple. It was glorious.

However, either as a joke or mistake, I was given the livelier of the two horses, and as soon as we began to trot, my horse took off galloping and jumping over ravines and bushes. I hung on to the saddle horn for dear life, pulling on the reins as hard as I could to get the horse to stop, practically having him on his two hind legs. Losing control of the running horse, I started screaming for help. Frank quickly rode up alongside me, yelling, "Throw me the reins!" I threw them as best I could and, just as if we were starring in a Western, he grabbed hold of the reins pulling the horse to a halt.

My hero. My cowboy. My Frank.

Because I'd been holding the saddle horn so tightly, the muscles in my hand had contracted and wouldn't loosen. When we got back to the hotel, my hand looked like a claw, and I tried to hide it in my jacket as we passed the other guests lying by the hotel pool.

In the room, while bathing my hand in warm water, I ruefully mentioned that at some point during my wild ride, a gold Tiffany money clip Frank had given me had popped out of my jacket pocket. I asked if we should go back to try and find it, but Frank, despite being unimpressed and I think embarrassed by my performance, just said, "Oh, don't worry about it. I'll buy you another one."

We never rode horses again.

The following day, thinking about the lost money clip that never had more than a dollar or two in it anyway, and the direction my life was going, I decided to raise something that had been on my mind for quite a while but had solidified as my New Year's resolution. Frank looked relaxed lying by the pool; it seemed like the perfect time to approach him. I nervously took a deep breath, then told him I was tired of working menial jobs and wanted to go to school to learn to be the fashion designer I'd always dreamed of being. I explained I'd discovered LA Trade Tech, a tuition-free school with a good design department in downtown Los Angeles, and could support myself with a job working nights and going to school days. Plus, the design course would be only one year! It was important to get the proper training because even though I could design and sketch, I still needed to learn how clothes were constructed. Whenever I'd shown people in the fashion industry my sketches, I'd been told they liked my designs but that I needed to learn how clothes were made.

Frank started sputtering, saying we would never see each other if I had that kind of schedule. I countered that we could still be together every weekend, hoping he understood my dilemma—and my ambitions.

The subject was dropped until breakfast the next morning when, suddenly, he said matter-of-factly, "OK! I've been thinking about what you said and have an idea. I'll tell you what. If I put money into your bank account each month to pay for your basic expenses, you won't have to work, and we can see more of each other. But! I want you to know that this is me helping you, not keeping you. That's essential, do you understand?"

I did, and I thanked him as genuinely as I could, feeling truly thankful that I could finally pursue one of my lifelong dreams. I told him my financial requirements and he said he would put seventy-five dollars in the account each month.

"Seventy-five dollars?" I echoed. "You weren't joking. You are definitely *not* keeping me!"

At that, we both laughed, and I gratefully hugged him.

With Frank's "blessing," I enrolled in LA Trade Tech. The school had technical courses teaching a wide range of classes in auto repair, cooking, machine shop, and dress design. The design class I chose was a two-year course, but I only opted for one year because I felt I already knew how to sketch and design clothes; what I didn't know was how clothes were made, so I wanted to learn how to sew, construct patterns, and resize them. All I'd be missing by not completing the entire course was an education in the basics of fashion and fabrics.

For most of the following year, I remained living where I was, taking the bus downtown to school and seeing Frank on weekends. Whenever I brought up the subject of us living together and perhaps cutting expenses, Frank would say he needed his privacy and couldn't imagine living with another person. (In later years, however, he told of having once shared a penthouse with Herbert May, C.E.O. of Westinghouse Airbrake in the Washington D.C. Statler Hotel during World War II, when he had been a captain in the Navy.)

After returning to the apartment from a weekend at Frank's, I'd often find my roommates had given large parties and my bed was unkempt, the whole place in disarray. Having roommates who were single party boys wasn't conducive to doing schoolwork, so I moved out to share a quiet one-bedroom with a sweet guy named Jimmy Putnam, each in our little single bed. I'd lie there at night wondering what Frank was up to, baffled at how we could be so close at times and yet so far apart at other times. I'd come to discover that was just the way it would always be with Frank. He was never consistently present in my life, and the times when we would spend longer amounts of time together revealed the inconsistencies of his emotional temperament, which was unpredictable at best and often downright critical.

During the 1950s, *Confidential* was a scandal magazine specializing in sordid stories about the private lives of famous people and Hollywood stars. The editor seemed to have a special penchant for trying to dig up dirt on my old friend Princess Radziwill, and he ultimately succeeded, publishing a scandalous article when she went to prison after being caught with drugs. The details in the article were mostly true as far as I could tell, but I felt so bad for her when I saw it, I couldn't bring myself to read the whole thing. It's a terrible feeling to know someone you care about fall so quickly from grace, and have it scathingly written in the press.

After Lois was released from prison, I received a telephone call from her begging me for help. She cried, saying she had little money and no place to live. Against my better judgment, I relented and suggested we meet.

My heart sank when I saw her. She had once been such a beautiful, confident woman. Now she looked dejected, with no spark left in her eyes. I suggested she stay with my parents and that we would try to figure something out for her, but I had no idea whether my parents would agree to it or if it was even a good idea.

I explained to them that Lois needed help without telling them about her drug habit, knowing they would have never understood the severity and would certainly not have accepted her into their modest duplex apartment on Ozone Avenue in Venice.

Dad was not impressed at all by Lois's title of Princess (and would jokingly refer to her as "Lowass" in private), but both my parents realized she was a flawed person in need of help. Even though Lois's own family lived nearby, she had severed ties with them long before, making it impossible for her to stay with them. Ultimately, my parents agreed, but they set a finite timeline for it and said she'd have to be out in three months.

I still remember seeing Lois that first night curled up on my parents' living room sofa, the only place for her to sleep. Here was the once fabulous and world-celebrated Princess Radziwill in borrowed pajamas sleeping on a tattered couch. It was almost unbelievable.

At one point, my sister Sandy suggested Lois rent an apartment with her in the Wilshire District, away from Lois's louche friends. Sandy, who often sewed her own clothes, even offered to make Lois a new wardrobe to help give her the confidence to begin her new life.

It all seemed to be working out famously until one Saturday morning when I received a phone call from a friend who said, "Have you seen the *Los Angeles Times*? If not, I suggest you go out immediately and get one."

I threw on some clothes and rushed to the corner newsstand, only to see this blaring headline:

PRINCESS AND LADY-IN-WAITING ARRESTED

The accompanying story was about Lois and my sister being arrested at the Wilshire apartment where, in the middle of the night, the police showed up to arrest Lois for dealing drugs and Sandy as an accomplice.

I was completely shocked and beside myself, wondering how on earth this could have happened right under our noses and after we'd been so generous to her. I immediately called a lawyer friend, Harry Weiss, asking for advice, and then I called Frank and told him everything. Frank had never been fond of my sister, but he set his feelings for her aside and said without hesitation that he would help me in any way he could. When Harry called back with the bail information, he said Sandy's bail would be $700. I called Frank again and we agreed to meet at the Beverly Hills Hotel, where they would cash a check for him on that weekend morning since the banks were closed.

When we arrived at the hotel, Frank kissed me on the cheek and handed me an envelope with the seven hundred dollars. I thanked him profusely, and then I borrowed Frank's car and drove downtown to the jail to meet the lawyer. When Sandy was led out from the holding cells, she was utterly shaken and crying.

Harry managed to convince the police that my sister was simply an unwitting friend of Lois, and all charges against her were dropped. Lois, on the other hand, was arraigned, with a trial date set a few weeks later at the Los Angeles County Courthouse. I decided to attend the trial and was sitting in the last row when the police officers brought Lois, handcuffed, into the courtroom. My eyes welled with tears seeing her wearing what had once been a beautiful white wool Christian Dior suit but was now yellowed and dirty, and on her head, a cheap straw boater hat. Her face was bloated and blotched. After a short proceeding, the judge sentenced the once-celebrated Princess Radziwill to two years in prison.

As the officers led her out, she turned to me and said with a wan smile, "Larry, don't ever get involved with people like me again."

Dazed and saddened seeing her downfall, I walked out of the courthouse, my mind flooded with memories. I never saw Lois again, but occasionally stories surfaced of sightings among mutual friends, none of them ever favorable. The last I heard, she had become a prostitute in New York, selling her body on the streets of Harlem. Lois died of a drug overdose in 1967, her once beautiful body covered in needle marks.

NINE

South Of The Border

Breaking a tradition of spending Christmas with his family in Sewickley, Pennsylvania, for the first time Frank and I decided to go to Mexico City to visit his friends Mary Rogers (daughter of humorist Will Rogers) and her gay best friend, George Weston. We had heard numerous stories and rumors about the petite, charming, and deceptively innocent Mary. George had known her since their school days in California. When she was in town, he was her protector and at her beck and call.

I first met Mary at Virginia Burrows's apartment, and we discovered we had a mutual friend, Princess Zina Rachevsky. Each year, Mary would return to Los Angeles for family business and I would see her at a cocktail party Virginia would give in her honor. Every year Mary would ask me the same question, "Larry, how is Zina?" My response would always be the same, "I haven't seen Zina in years." Just before Mary arrived for her annual visit I'd read a book about Zina, and when Mary asked me the same question, I said, "Mary, Zina became a nun and died in the Himalayas." She never mentioned Zina again.

For years Frank and I had heard stories of Mary's outrageous habit of drunkenly picking fights in bars with strange men and then bringing them home for sex games. We already knew she'd been asked to leave Athens, Greece for that kind of behavior, so her move to Mexico was a logical choice where we figured at least she'd be unknown.

When Frank and I got to Mexico, we spent time touring the city with Mary and George, eating at a different restaurant each night before hitting the bars, but with a watchful eye on Mary. Nothing dramatic happened while we were there, but we were all holding our breath just waiting for Mary to act out. She seemed perfectly normal, which is still to this day completely bewildering to me given what we'd soon come to find out.

Big drama had always been a part of Mary Rogers' life. She'd behaved well while we were with her, but something had to happen. And it did.

Frank and I had left Mary and George in Mexico City and rented a car to drive to Acapulco and spend New Year's Eve alone. We stopped in Cuernavaca for a couple of nights on the way to Acapulco, and that's when we heard the shocking news that Mary's latest Mexican boyfriend had been found dead in her apartment and that both she and George had fled the country. Unbelievable. We'd *just* been with them, and neither of them showed any signs of suspicion or distress. How could this have all happened?

Poor George, we thought. Always so loyal to Mary—but this time there was real trouble. We immediately wondered if he returned with her to Los Angeles or followed her wherever she ended up going, and those questions and many more consumed us as we continued to Acapulco for our New Year's Eve celebration. It was such a surreal turn of events, and we had no means of communication to get more of the story.

1955. Mexico City. I cut Frank out of the picture
after one of our numerous quarrels.
From the author's collection.

Acapulco was exciting and beautiful. Nearly naked local boys dove into the water off a cliff next to a hotel where we dined in a candlelit restaurant alongside Lana Turner, Arlene Dahl, and Merle Oberon, all glittering in jewels. The white beaches were crowded with golden bodies while the deep blue Pacific lapped at the shore. Our hotel, Las Brisas, provided us with a pink Jeep to explore the countryside. It was heaven, and before we knew it, we'd all but forgotten about Mary Rogers and poor innocent George.

On our last evening, we were invited to a party on a small island only accessible by ferry from the nearby wharf. The lanterns in the trees lit the dancing couples and the margaritas flowed. For me, they flowed a bit too easily, and soon I was led by the hand of a tall and seductive Mexican man to the far side of the small island. Frank saw what was occurring and immediately ran towards us, pulling me away from the man and saying we were leaving. Without much success, I drunkenly blathered some excuse about the man only wanting to show me the sights, much to Frank's dismay.

I was suffering from a hangover in bed the next morning (and not wanting to face Frank after the night before) when the hotel room suddenly began to shake. We heard a commotion on the walkway outside and men were shouting *"El temblor! El temblor!"* Of course, why not add an earthquake to our Mexican adventure? If anything can cut through a hangover, it's an earthquake. In an instant, we threw on our clothes, grabbed our suitcases, got into a taxi, and made it to the airport, dodging fallen trees and rutted roads the entire way.

Finally able to catch our breaths, we took our seats on the plane and ordered a couple of cocktails. I was just happy to be alive and getting out of Mexico so soon, but when I tried to apologize to Frank, it was clear that he was still angry with me from the previous night. He could barely look at me and didn't speak a word until we were back in Los Angeles.

I wasn't the only one who might have misbehaved and been unthinking at times. Frank could be unkind and belittling, like criticizing me whenever I played his Steinway piano and saying I made too many mistakes. After his repeated harping about my playing, I finally got so upset that I never again touched his piano even though it was one of my life's great joys.

At times, his comments about the way I dressed or conducted myself made me cry. He'd then accuse me of being too sensitive or claim that I couldn't take a joke. After one of those episodes, I ran out the door and down the hill to my Clark Street apartment. My next-door neighbors, Alan and Phyllis Sues, were sitting outside their apartment and invited me in for a strong slug of whiskey when they saw how distraught I was. They were both very funny comedians who performed in nightclubs all over the country and their jokes and experiences had me laughing in minutes, completely forgetting what had transpired. As the saying goes, "Laughter certainly is the best medicine."

There was another Frank, though—one who was kind and caring. He always picked up dinner checks and gave money to friends who were unable to work due to their age, regularly donated to charities, and if I ever tried to pay, would casually brush it off, saying, "Oh, don't worry, Larry, there's more where that came from."

I never really thought about his money considering he lived in a simply furnished house, dressed during the day in faded Levis, drove a 1948 Oldsmobile, and in the evenings wore a well-worn blue blazer. Even his Charvet silk bathrobe was tattered. When my friends would tease me about catching a very rich man, I said I was certain he was comfortable but not rich. No, it wasn't until years later when I needed a loan and had no alternative that I asked for money. I would have rather waited until the eleventh hour before telling him of my predicament, but when I did, he immediately provided the needed funds, saying he thought I was a good risk and would promptly repay the debt.

There was a lot of good and a lot of not-so-good with Frank. But he still had my heart, and I do believe, despite his nastiness, that I had his. It was a complicated relationship. I'm not sure we ever saw eye to eye, given the many disagreements we had and the number of times he'd blatantly ignore me in public or pretend like I wasn't his other half around certain company. Perhaps it was a matter of clinging to his independence, so he could continue living his footloose and fancy-free lifestyle, which, I'm aware, allowed him the freedom to sleep with whomever he wanted, whenever he wanted. We fell into a don't-ask, don't-tell routine, which was fine by me even though I'd have preferred to have had him all to myself.

But at the end of the day, you can't change anyone but yourself. I decided it was better to have a piece of him than to have nothing at all, so I learned how to deal with his proclivities and less favorable traits and did my best to protect myself from his verbal and emotional abuse.

TEN

Poor Little Rich Boy

Frank hadn't explored his sexuality until he was thirty-two years old, having had only two short affairs with men his age. Then, at just shy of forty-two, he met me, someone twenty years his junior whose sexuality was rumbling, who was very independent, and who wanted a career as a dress designer. He was totally at a loss about how to handle or understand our relationship. Because of his inexperience, even his lovemaking was limited and often unsatisfying.

After his death, I read diaries from his Princeton years that even then complained of excessive drinking and hangovers. Frank was what's known as a functioning alcoholic; his drinking was not obvious to others, but there was many a night driving us home he'd be so drunk that he'd steer with one eye open and pass out as soon as we reached the driveway. Early in our dating, the first time it happened, I thought, *oh my God, this guy had a heart attack!* On our first date together, I had tried to match him drink for drink, but when he dropped me off at my apartment after dinner, I was so drunk I couldn't even find the lock to the door. So, yes, there were many reasons we were often incompatible—and I knew a few from the beginning—but, strangely enough, we loved one another.

Frank Martin Tack was born in 1911 in Oil City, Pennsylvania, where the first commercial oil wells in America were dug in 1859. His Episcopal family owned an oil company and eventually moved to Sewickley, a wealthy suburb of Pittsburgh. He grew up with people like the famous Mellon banking family, went to the finest private schools, belonged to the best clubs (No Jews, no Catholics, please), and graduated in 1935 from Princeton University. Upon graduating, he was gifted a year's trip around the world, what is today known as a gap year, before starting a career. But he never quite made it into the workforce. Frank was "old money" but never gave an impression of wealth. He simultaneously disdained yet took advantage of the upper-class life he had. Frank preferred a more bohemian lifestyle, such as recording famous jazz singers in his room at Princeton (we were at a jazz club in Los Angeles when the singer Sarah Vaughn spotted Frank, came to our table, hugged him, and said, "Frank baby, I have not seen you since the '40s"). Or, when in New York, going to the Harlem jazz clubs. However, Frank's father still controlled the purse strings and to a degree limited Frank's financial independence even though he was living on the interest of a trust given to him by an aunt.

When we first met, I asked what kind of work he did, and he said his only work was making himself happy. I had never known anyone who didn't have to work for a living, but Frank spent his days tinkering in his at-home "lab" with electronic equipment, listening to music, and reading periodicals. It wasn't until our relationship became serious that his family history was slowly leaked. His friends were a mixture of the well-to-do, plus jazz, Broadway, and movie musicians among other interesting working folks (he bought his first

Los Angeles house from the two composers of the Broadway hits *Song of Norway* and *Kismet*). He enjoyed surrounding himself with people he said amused him. His closest friend, Philip May, grew up with Frank and it was Philip's equally gay father, Herb, with whom Frank had shared the D.C. penthouse.

There were few women in his social life save for the enduring friendship with Virginia Burrows, and because of me, a lovely twenty-something English girl, Joan Weber. The two women often acted as our "beards" whenever a social situation required it, as so often they did in the '50s.

I'd like to think that Frank's wealth had no bearing on my attraction to him or on his attitude toward me, but with the passage of time, I've come to realize that money has a way of coloring any relationship, regardless of how "pure" or honest one's intentions are. While it may not have been something either of us had initially sought out in each other, our upbringings couldn't have been more different. Frank, coming from old money and privilege, and me, coming from the projects and poverty. This of course played out in our relationship from time to time and in complex ways. It presented as a power dynamic, where Frank's social life would supersede mine, or we would go where he wanted to go and eat where he wanted to eat. I can see now that this took its toll on me over time; it steadily eroded my sense of self and compromised who I was since in the end, he was the one with the power.

ELEVEN

Misbehavin'

Among Frank's friends were two Hawaiian brothers, one of whom was an aspiring nightclub singer who lived in Benedict Canyon. One summer evening, they threw a luau for about forty gay men, flying in leis from Hawaii and roasting a pig. All evening, none other than Liberace sat playing the upright piano while the rest of the guests mingled and got drunk on Mai Tais. After drinking one too many myself, I became ill and went into the small bathroom where I vomited and passed out on the floor, resting my head against the cool toilet base.

The next thing I knew, I woke to the sound of Frank pounding on the bathroom door, yelling, "Who are you in there with?"

When I didn't respond, he forced the door open by lowering his shoulder and throwing all his weight into it. When it busted open, I was lying on the floor, unable to even look up at him. Furious, he dragged me out of the house, saying he would never take me to another party.

Of course, this turned out to be an empty threat. A similar

situation happened when we were at another boozy late-night party, this time on the beach at Dana Point. I had drunkenly wandered off with another guy and we passed out in each other's arms with the surf lapping at our feet. Frank finally found us and aggressively pulled me up, dragged me across the sand, and shoved me into the car. At every red light on the way home, he'd slam on the brakes, causing me to fall forward and hit my head on the dashboard.

Although Frank was an alcoholic, unlike me, he rarely showed the effects of being drunk in public. It was only when we were home that I would experience his drunken behavior. He never took a drink until 7 p.m., but after dinner, drinking until he passed out around 2 a.m., he'd read magazines while slowly sipping almost an entire bottle of Scotch whiskey. When he turned sixty-five, he decided he couldn't handle Scotch anymore and started drinking beer instead, even with dinner. At home, he changed his nighttime drinking habit to a bottle of Dom Perignon champagne. That was Frank's idea of not drinking.

In the 1950s, gay bars were few and far between. At the ones that did exist, an active police squad was often ready to pounce at any "offense," such as a simple touch on the shoulder of a person of the same sex, or God forbid a hug. San Francisco seemed to be more open, with bars like the Black Cat where one could drink, dance, and dine with abandon. We began flying up to San Francisco and checking into the Huntington Hotel on Nob Hill, where Frank had not only stayed during World War II but had once been thrown out of in the middle of the night because of an episode with a sailor he'd picked up. The sailor awakened during the night and had to pee; instead of opening the bathroom door, he opened the outer, door only to be discovered naked in the hallway by the night manager. In a matter of minutes, the hotel management unceremoniously threw

Frank and his inamorata out at 4 a.m.!

Driving back to the Huntington one night after leaving a party, Frank and I began arguing about his paying too much attention to someone earlier. When he stopped at a red light, I jumped out in a fit of anger, slammed the door, and walked to the hotel. By the time I arrived, he'd passed out in bed. Standing over him, I was still so mad I thought about what it would feel like to hit him over the head with the bedside lamp, but then I realized the lamp was made of cork so it would only break at best, and I would end up not only paying for it but having to hear Frank berate me for one more thing. So, yet again, I undressed and climbed into bed next to him and hoped it would all go away.

We found hotel life inconvenient and started looking for a rental pied-à-terre in North Beach. Val, a decorator friend, had moved to San Francisco from Los Angeles, whereupon he changed his last name from Anastasia to the more anglicized Arnold and became a successful decorator to the rich. He began to look for apartments we might like and ultimately found us a tiny railroad flat at the corner of Greenwich and Grant that cost only fifty dollars a month. We kept that place for twenty years, still paying the original rental price until Frank bought his apartment. The North Beach flat was so small Frank's artist friend Loring Hayden flew out from New York and painted a large trompe l'oeil mural on the living room wall to give the impression of a window overlooking a garden. We used to joke that the apartment was so small that if you wanted to change your mind, you had to walk outside.

TWELVE

Chance In A Lifetime

My friend Paul Whitney had just returned from Paris where he had been a design apprentice at the couture studio of Balenciaga. To celebrate, we went to the very popular Sunset Boulevard restaurant Frascati. Since I had neglected to reserve a table ahead of time, we were asked to wait in a long line of guests. The line moved slowly, and I noticed directly in front of us an acquaintance, "Doc," accompanied by an impeccably dressed and slight man: the famous Greek American dress designer James Galanos. We all introduced ourselves and decided it would probably be easier to be seated at a table for four than wait for the limited tables of two, which turned out to be the case.

Once we were seated and had ordered drinks, Paul began to regale us with tales of interning at Balenciaga, me trying to get a word in edgewise to let them know I was a student of dress design, and both Mr. Galanos and "Doc" left with little opportunity to say anything at all. After lots of wine and a good dinner, we exchanged telephone numbers, and that chance encounter was the beginning of wonderful new relationships: for Paul and Jimmy, who soon there-after would start dating, and for me, who would later be offered the opportunity of a lifetime.

A few days later I called Jimmy and invited him for a drink and to meet my partner Frank, which he was more than happy to do. At that meeting, we realized we had many friends in common and began socializing together in the weeks and months ahead.

Always interested in the ongoing conversation, Jimmy rarely spoke of himself. After a while, I came to understand that his silence was not only because he was a good listener, but because underneath it all, there was a loneliness inside of him that was yearning for more connection. Once I realized that, I made more of an effort to befriend him. On my free nights, I would meet him at Will Wright's, a quaint ice cream parlor on the Sunset Strip just down the hill from his Regency-style house. I would pepper him with questions and listen in fascination to how he began his career and his well-defined ideas and philosophy of good design. He, in turn, would ask about my schooling and my plans for my future. Never once did he ask me about Frank. It was a collegial and professional friendship, but also relaxed and warm. I was so grateful to be in his company and to be able to absorb all his industry insight and experience.

One evening, he asked if I would like to show him some of the designs from the portfolio I was building to find a design industry job once I finished school. The following day, I brought the sketches to his Sepulveda Boulevard offices with my heart pounding, anticipating showing the master my work. After slowly looking at them, he smiled and, in a measured voice, paid me a great compliment.

"You do not belong in Los Angeles," he said. "You belong in New York."

"But-but-but," I stammered, "I don't have the money to go to New York."

"Don't worry about it," he said. "I will think of something."

1956. Jimmy Galanos was testing his new camera and shot a series of photographs of me in different costumes.
From the author's collection.

The next time we met, he said he had an idea: Since he would be showing his upcoming collection at the Plaza Hotel in New York, he would introduce me to people in the industry if I agreed to dress the models and assist in sales each day.

Here was the opportunity I'd been waiting for my whole life. It would be a chance to network and an introduction to the dress capital of America from none other than Jimmy Galanos. And the best part was there were no strings attached. I'd already understood the "no strings" because Jimmy was madly in love with Paul, and he and I had never had an inkling of romantic interest in each other.

When I told Frank, he was furious and said Jimmy probably wanted to get into my pants, which I vehemently denied, explaining this was a golden chance for me to begin the career I had dreamt of for so long. I told Frank he could live with me in New York if things went as planned. Then, shortly after I decided to accept Jimmy's invitation to New York, Frank presented me with a shiny new black and white Corvette convertible. In the back of my mind, I knew that it was a not-so-subtle bribe for me to stay.

Frank finally relented, and a few weeks later I flew with Jimmy to New York, where we had a large two-room suite at the Plaza for the entire month of June.

When I was an eighteen-year-old with only one dollar in my pocket, I would stand at the Plaza's Oak Room bar and nurse my drink, looking at all the glamorous people chattering away. Now, here I was, staying at that same hotel. Upon arrival in the Oak Room, I was warmly greeted by the maître d' and seated at a prime table. As that teen, often before I entered the Oak Room, I sat on one of the tiny gold chairs in the lobby watching the well-dressed guests enter through the revolving doors, wondering who they were and wishing I were one of them. Now, each time I entered those same revolving doors, I looked around the lobby searching for that boy who was mesmerized by the ever-passing parade of sophisticated New York life.

That year, *Town and Country* magazine honored Galanos at a black-tie dinner and dance on the roof of the St. Regis Hotel and gave him four impossible-to-get tenth-row tickets to the hottest Broadway show in New York: *My Fair Lady*. Jimmy invited the model Pat Jones, his close friend Arthur Englander (a Merchandise

Manager from Neiman Marcus Dallas), and me. I didn't own a tuxedo, but Jimmy had brought an extra one. Even though he was shorter and slimmer than me, he thought we could make the suit fit if I kept the pants pulled down on my hips, the jacket buttoned, and my hands in my pockets in order not to show the too-short sleeves.

The following day, I went to Bloomingdale's to buy a white dress shirt, black bow tie, and black patent leather shoes. On the big evening, the four of us were whisked by a limousine to and from the theater. The show itself was superb, and we all left with a skip in our step. Then, when we entered the rooftop restaurant at the hotel, an orchestra immediately struck up the hit song from the show we'd just seen: "On the Street Where You Live." It was an extraordinarily exciting moment in the life of a kid who'd grown up dreaming of such things in the projects in Minneapolis. I was home in the world at last.

Through Jimmy's contacts, I headed out on interviews with my design portfolio in hand. One was with an austere-looking woman at the firm of Anna Miller & Co. After perusing my sketches, she kindly asked if I would like to become a design assistant to the designer Bill Blass. *An assistant?* I thought. *Not me, I am a designer!* In Los Angeles, an assistant was the lowest position in a design company and was known as "picking up pins." Naively thinking that's the kind of job it was, I thanked her for her offer and said I would consider the position—which of course I then refused, making one of the biggest errors of my dress design career.

In retrospect, I could have learned so much that I'd missed out on in my single year of formal education, but it wasn't to be. We all make mistakes along the way, and I'm just grateful that I was given other opportunities to make up for some of my missteps. In my head and my heart, I was a designer.

Luckily, I was hired soon after by a firm called Highlight Fashions in the Garment District to replace the current designer and give the collection a more youthful look. It wasn't even close to the same caliber as working as an assistant to Bill Blass, but it was a design job.

I returned to the Plaza ecstatically informing Jimmy of my new job, which would require me to create a collection of black crepe dresses in less than a month. I began furiously sketching and Jimmy graciously helped me edit the sketches down to the required total of six dresses, making invaluable suggestions and gently guiding me while still allowing my authentic vision and skills to come through. Right out of school and here I was a New York designer. I couldn't believe it.

Four-ninety-eight, 530, and 560 Seventh Avenue were three addresses each with a different level of women's clothing manufacturers such as Anna Miller, Norman Norell, Donald Brooks, Pauline Trigere, and many others known and not so well known. All of them worked in one of these three buildings. My new design job was with Highlight Fashions in the least prestigious 498 building. Having no experience in the industry, I knew I was in over my head, so each morning leaving the elevator I would silently repeat the words my mother had taught me all those years ago when Dad changed our name to make it sound less Jewish: "Larry . . . *Fake it!*"

I quickly picked up the routine and began designing black crepe dresses for early fall delivery. In my design room, there were six sample sewers, an assistant for me, and a full-time "house" model who loved to walk around the factory naked except for panties, a display that tantalized and terrorized the male fabric cutters.

The first small collection was a hit. That fall, my little black crepe dresses were in all the windows of the store Tailored Woman at 57th Street and Fifth Avenue and were perfect for Jewish women to wear to the synagogue on the High Holidays. I called them "Back to Shul dresses," a play on "back-to-school."

When they appeared in the store, I telephoned my aunt Ethel and told her she should go and choose one she liked, then I'd take down the style number and get it for her at wholesale. I was so proud of my first major design, I couldn't wait to share it with her.

Her reply was, "When are you going to get a real job like a salesman in your uncle Lou's clothing store?"

"I'm not going to spend my life behind a counter," I retorted. "I'm a designer!"

But with the first collection finished, I wondered what I was supposed to do next. Without knowledge of the fabric market and what exactly was expected of me, I was soon let go—another reason I should have taken the Bill Blass assistant job. It was one of my first big lessons in fashion. As they say about the industry on the hit TV show *Project Runway*, "One day you're in, and the next day you're out." After my first big accomplishment, suddenly I was out, and it was time to find my next job.

During that time, Frank and I began writing to one another, but he rarely asked about my career. During the few phone calls we had, the conversation was usually strained, so I opted to write letters instead, to which he'd respond with only three to five sentences on a postcard.

After I lost my first job, I wound up sharing an apartment with my sister Sandy, who was designing sportswear for the company Evan-Picone. Without any furniture, Sandy slept in the living room on an army cot, and I slept on the bedroom floor wrapped in a hundred and twenty yards of a curly fabric called Poodle Cloth. Our dining table was a collapsible ironing board that collapsed one memorable evening during dinner.

For Christmas, Frank sent a telegram informing me of a waiting gift at an address on Fifth Avenue. Almost out of money, I hoped the address might be a bank and the gift a check. The next morning, I ran across town looking for the designated address, only to discover that it wasn't a bank but a typewriter store, where I was handed a very expensive Italian Olivetti typewriter. It was gorgeous, and I felt flattered that he'd spent so much money on me but disappointed that it wasn't exactly helpful given my current situation. When I called to thank him, he said the reason he sent a typewriter was that when I wrote him letters, he couldn't read my handwriting—a prime example of Frank's insensitivity to my taste or requirements.

For birthdays when I was in LA, he would tell me to just go out and choose whatever I wanted. One of those times, when he asked what I would like, I replied in my best Bette Davis voice, "How about some stock!"

Sure enough, the next day, he handed me shares of General Motors. It was a good call on my part because I hung on to that stock until many years later when I needed money and sold it for a handsome return. Whenever I gave him a gift, it was usually a sweater or some other clothing item. It was always a problem because he didn't wear jewelry and had everything else.

I started looking for another job and discovered that networking through contacts with other designers and people in the trade was the best way to find one. I hung out at the 498-building's downstairs restaurant where, on one side, sat the old European manufacturers and, on the other side, sat the designers.

I finally found a job at Lisa Kaye, a company making the most expensive maternity dresses in New York. The owners were a thirty-something couple, both very attractive. Each morning they would arrive at the office and practically fight to be first to use the full-length mirror, making sure their hair was just right.

I learned a lot on the job designing dresses where the shape was the same but the fabrics and trim varied. But I soon grew bored with maternity wear, and in less than nine months—no pun intended—I took another position designing junior dresses for a happening company named Sabrina. This time, I would only have one sample sewer and no assistant.

The first morning I was to report for work at Sabrina, I was walking to my subway stop on Madison Avenue when I suddenly felt dizzy and collapsed on the sidewalk. Before I could even begin my latest job, I was diagnosed with mononucleosis and confined to bed. My new boss told me not to worry and that the job would be there for me as soon as I got well, but little did I know how poor the working conditions would be once I did start. If I hadn't been so broke, I wouldn't have stayed there more than a week, but desperate times call for desperate measures, so I chalked it up to a "character-building" experience.

The truth was, I missed Frank. In each letter, I pleaded with him to come to New York. After a few months, he finally acquiesced and subleased a charming one-bedroom brownstone apartment on East 80th Street from his friend Loring, who was temporarily moving to Vermont. The apartment was located near the Metropolitan Museum and Central Park. It was only a short walk to the subway with a direct line to my job, and to top it off, we were living together!

Every year, Frank dutifully went to Sewickley, Pennsylvania, to spend Christmas with his parents and his sister Lois, whom he loathed. In all our years together, we never spent a Christmas or New Year together, save the one trip to Mexico. Alone for Christmas Eve in the apartment on East 80th Street, I decided to throw a party for friends of ours who had stayed in town for the holidays. Among the twelve guests were the singer Bobby Short, drink in hand, legs crossed, sitting in a red "telephone" chair looking very elegant, and Edelgy Dinshaw, a fey East Indian mogul wearing jeweled shoes. Edelgy was quite the sight to behold. Christmas music was playing, snow was falling outside, and I was serving potent martinis as the small crowd chatted happily. It was nearly perfect, except for one detail: the absence of Frank. No matter how strong the martinis were, or how beautiful the snow outside the window, or how much laughter filled the room, none of it made up for the fact that the man I loved more than anyone else in the world was never around during "the most wonderful time of the year." I learned how to manage without him, so in some ways it got easier, but I was never comfortable with it. I missed him on holidays as much as I'd missed him before he'd moved to New York. It just never seemed right that we couldn't be together for the holidays.

After the New Year, I lost yet another design job. Each had lasted longer than the one before it, but since I had so little training and scant idea of how to buy fabrics or shop for supplies, each one became an on-the-job learning experience. Sooner or later, my bosses would get tired of always having to catch me up to speed and decide that it was more efficient for their business to let me go than to invest the time and energy in training me. Unemployed, I'd go to Seventh Avenue every morning to interview for another coveted position, sometimes even showing up with my portfolio but without a scheduled interview, hoping for a miracle. Or, I'd lunch with other designers, choosing the cheapest thing on the menu and praying they might have a fresh tip about an open position somewhere. My methods proved futile and over the next four months, I began to lose hope.

Each evening, Frank grilled me on my daily activities, demanding to know how I was spending my time, not believing I was job hunting even though I had been. I would attempt to explain how one looked for a job in an industry without employment agencies or newspapers want ads but with little success. I was already disheartened and coming home to Frank's heavy-handed interrogations compounded all my negative feelings about my self-worth at the time. I'm not sure how I managed to summon any resolve during that dark period. Maybe it was the optimism of youth still burning somewhere inside me, or maybe it was the fear of having to return to the life of my childhood; whatever the reason, I kept on plugging away, bit by bit, day by day, knowing that my angels would eventually find me again and lead me to safety as long as I continued putting myself out there.

By that point, I was running out of savings, and my pride kept me from asking Frank for money. In an act of desperation, I took the Olivetti typewriter he'd given me for my birthday to a pawn shop on 57th Street and sold it, giving me just enough to cover my expenses until my next unemployment check arrived. It was a Hail Mary, and it worked. I got through until my next job started. The only problem was that I'd have to keep it a secret from Frank and could only hope that he wouldn't notice the typewriter had gone missing.

It wasn't all doom and gloom with Frank, though. Despite our frequent arguments, there were many times when we enjoyed one another's company. We were still, after all, in love with one another. On Frank's dime, we dined at excellent restaurants, went to Broadway plays and concerts, and shopped together.

I'll never forget one night at Lincoln Center, where we'd shown up for a Ravel charity event. Ravel was Frank's and my favorite composer, and the evening included a post-performance buffet dinner for donors in the Great Entry Hall. As we walked into the

Hall, we saw Lauren Bacall push her way to the front of the buffet line. And just as soon as we'd entered, we turned and left because Frank said he didn't want to eat with "those kinds of rude people." We headed straight to a restaurant across the street and had a fabulous dinner à deux. So, we knew we could be happy together at times, but it was never easy. Frank was too complicated of a character, and I'm sure he might have said the same about me.

Incidentally, years later at Bobby Short's seventieth birthday party, I ran into Lauren Bacall and told her the story about the Ravel evening. She looked me straight in the eye and said, "Well, I was hungry!"

At the end of those difficult four months, I found a job, and Frank decided to move back to his house in California, claiming he had business commitments to take care of. I told Frank I would miss him but understood his decision. In passing, he then turned and wryly said since I'd always liked Bobby Short so much, maybe I should call him.

And that's exactly what I did. A few days after Frank left, I called Bobby and asked him to dinner. Then I panicked, realizing I had never been alone with him and figuring that because he was so sophisticated, he'd find any conversation with me boring. I'm not sure if I did it to spite Frank or because I was truly attracted to Bobby. Either way, I worried that I'd gotten in over my head by inviting him to dinner, so I quickly called the few people I knew in the city to make it more of a group dinner than a date, but everyone was busy that evening, so a "date" it was.

Bobby came for a cocktail looking very elegant in a bespoke plaid sports jacket with a Hermès handkerchief flopping casually out of his breast pocket. We grabbed a cab and went to dinner at one of our favorite New York restaurants, Le Veau d'Or. As soon as we sat down at the table, Bobby immediately sensed my uneasiness, just as he had at our first meeting in Los Angeles.

"Isn't this nice," he said, trying to calm my nerves. "Just the two of us. We finally have a chance to talk."

It was at once disarming, flirty and relaxed me. We laughed and talked until we were the last guests in the restaurant. From that night on, there would always be a little rumble going on between us, and whenever we crossed paths, I'd feel it, but it never went any further until many years later after Frank died.

When the lease on the brownstone was up, and without another apartment lined up, I temporarily took a small room in the Madison Hotel. Many people referred to it as the "Home for Broken Broads" because it was known as a haven for divorced ladies, and I certainly felt like one of them.

Frank and I were still technically together, but the commuting and long-distance situation became increasingly difficult, so I began to put out feelers for a job in Los Angeles. The well-known designer Donald Brooks had told me that if I wanted to make it big in New York I would have to wine, dine, and lunch with buyers and editors regularly. "Make it your second job, if not your first," he said, "to get in front of them at all costs." As soon as he said it, I immediately knew it wasn't the life for me. My private life was more important than that, and Frank was a major part of that life, even if it was currently fractured by distance.

On one of my trips back to LA, I was interviewed and hired on the spot by Pat Premo, a 1930s pioneer in California fashion. She decided she wanted to cut her workload and hired me as a co-designer. I returned to New York and resigned from my position, then headed back to California to live with Frank.

1957. I designed the dress for an Italian wine promotion.
Copyright unknown. From the author's collection.

When I returned to Los Angeles, I found a changed Jimmy Galanos who was no longer friendly. His boyfriend Paul had convinced him that he was now the Great Galanos and didn't need lowly people like me around. We were simply written out of his life. Now he ran with the movie stars he dressed, such as Rosalind

Russell, Jennifer Jones, and society ladies Betsy Bloomingdale and Nancy Reagan, among others. Jimmy fell for it hook, line, and sinker, and even his closest friend, the designer Gustave Tassell, would be required to address him as "James" from that point forward. My old friend Jimmy had fully transformed into *James Galanos*, complete with a whole new affect, including a European pronunciation of his last name.

After a few years, his affair with Paul ended, and then my telephone rang. It was Jimmy. We renewed our friendship and being the kind, sweet, and unassuming person he had always been with friends and celebrities alike, Jimmy returned to his old self once again, inquiring about my career and foibles and laughing at all the recent gossip. Still, he told me little of his career and certainly nothing of his love life, which I always found curious. Our evenings together resumed, however, and slowly our friendship deepened.

THIRTEEN

It's My Life

The Corvette convertible Frank had given me was waiting to whisk me to my new job. I felt happy being back in LA with him and life was rosy. I zoomed to work from Beverly Hills to the MacArthur Park district in less than twenty minutes. One evening while coming home, I was stopped by a cop who told me he'd been watching me speed faster and faster each night on the same street. I explained I'd never had a ticket before, that I was sorry, and pleaded with him not to give me a fine. He looked at my driver's license and then asked me for my telephone number, which I readily gave.

"Okay, this time you can go," he said, handing my license back to me. "But please slow down. If it happens again, I'll have to write you a ticket."

Breathing a sigh of relief, I drove home, where I promptly told Frank about the incident and how lucky I'd been. "But why do you think he asked for our phone number?"

"Are you crazy?" Frank admonished me. "You gave him our telephone number? If he calls, I am going to tell him off."

It had never occurred to me that there could be a gay cop out there. Happily, I never heard from him, but it wouldn't be the last time I got reprimanded by Frank. Far from it.

New problems arose when I told Frank I couldn't go out to dinner or parties during the week because I needed to prepare sketches for the next day's work, and I had to go to bed at a decent hour to be fresh for work in the morning. Meanwhile, Frank's drinking continued. When he'd come home late, he would inevitably awaken me, which nearly always resulted in an argument. We fought so often that I moved into one of the downstairs bedrooms, but even after that, it finally reached the point where living together became untenable.

Frank's drinking made him the quintessential Dr. Jekyll and Mr. Hyde. The night before I moved out, he came home so drunk and angry he started banging on the locked bedroom door, threatening to kill me. The next morning, while I was packing to leave, he calmly and charmingly said, "Do you realize what you're giving up, Larry?" I'd fallen for it before, hoping he might change when we talked things out, when he was sober and lucid, but this time something was different. A line had been crossed and there was no turning back. Evidently, after years together, he still could not understand who I was or why we were together. I knew I had to leave to save myself.

When I walked out of the house for the last time, I left the Corvette in the garage, understanding that the true ownership was not in my name, but, as I'd feared, a bribe to get me to behave as Frank would have wished.

I bought a '57 Ford Fairlane and moved into an apartment above a storefront on noisy Melrose Avenue. When friends asked about the sounds from the street, I said it was just like being in New York. Alone for another Christmas, one of the neighbors invited me to a party where I met Jerry Furlow, a sweet guy who'd just arrived from Oklahoma. Jerry was a blue-eyed innocent with a crew cut and an accent barely decipherable to me, the "sophisticate." We began to date shortly thereafter and, coming off the heels of an affair with a man twenty years older, I found being with a person my age was surprisingly fun and easy. I was able to share my lifestyle and my friends, and we had a lot in common. Jerry and I became boyfriends and after a year together rented a small house, bought a Kerry Blue puppy, and were happily living as a couple.

Meanwhile, Frank would occasionally call and ask if we could just have dinner together, forcing me to explain to him over and over again that I was now with Jerry. It seemed like no matter how much I'd changed or how much time had passed, Frank was always right there trying to reel me back in, testing my resolve.

AH MEN (The Store)

Jerry and I were sitting at the dining room table, and I was teaching him to sew a chocolate brown linen swimsuit on the miniature Singer sewing machine I'd had in design school. Most of the suit was finished but before putting in the lining and adding the contrasting cream-colored waistband, I asked him to try it on. The unfinished suit hugged his slim hips, looking hot and sexy. We decided to leave it as it was without the band. "Besides," I said, "it's easier to finish this way." A tight waistband on swimwear was the norm, but without it, this one looked new and different.

At the time, Jerry and I were both working in the fashion industry in downtown Los Angeles. He was a sales representative for a sportswear company, and I was designing cocktail dresses for a different company. Each day, we drove together to our respective jobs, and on one rainy morning, Jerry confessed to me how unhappy he was with his sales job and how he had always dreamed of opening a clothing store. Laughing and fantasizing that the store would be for men and women, I suggested we should call the store "Ah Men, Ah Women"—after the name of a current Broadway play.

Each time Jerry wore the linen hip-hugging swimsuit on the beach in Santa Monica, he was showered with compliments, prompting us to tell a couple of friends about his idea of opening a store that sold this type of swimwear. We had no idea how we'd do it, and having little money, it seemed an impossible pipe dream. However, more and more of our friends thought a store was a great idea, and before we knew it, they offered to contribute seed money to help turn our fantasy into a reality. Pooling our meager funds, we managed to raise $1200.

It was almost a year to the exact day when Jerry had first told me about his idea that our dream came true, and we opened the doors to our new store on the corner of Melrose and Robertson in West Hollywood. It was just as we'd imagined minus one small detail: the Ah Women part never made it into the name. The bathing suit I'd sewn on our dining room table, and that Jerry had made "famous" on Will Rogers State Beach in Santa Monica, became the iconic AH MEN trademark.

The 1960s ushered in The Peacock Revolution, an exciting moment in men's fashion that cast aside the current and former trends in favor of flamboyant and radical new looks, attitudes, and influences. Carnaby Street and Kings Road in London were the epicenters of the movement, thanks to the meteoric rise of The Beatles. Shoulder-length hair became the new rage, resembling the cartoon character Prince Valiant, along with collarless jackets, tighter pants, and colorful, wild shirts. But in the early '60s, the revolution had yet to hit America, and even in forward-thinking California men were still dressing in the same uninspired way as they had in the 1950s and before.

There were, however, a few creators exploring new fashion roads. Among them were Gene Burkhard and his secretary, who were dying jockstraps in vibrant colors out of a garage in San Diego. That endeavor would ultimately become the International Male store and catalog. At about the same time, Parr of Arizona was another small successful company showing sexy swimwear geared to a more adventurous gay customer.

Jerry and I ended our romance but decided to remain friends and go ahead with the planned retail partnership. We had a hunch we were onto something great and didn't want anything to get in the way of that. I had no intention of giving up my design career, so I offered to help in any way I could, knowing it was a great opportunity just to be nominally involved.

West Hollywood was our intended locale. We looked for a space to rent and found a small room on the second floor of a 1920s two-story wooden complex on San Vicente Boulevard where the Pacific Design Center now stands. The building's tenants were struggling creative entrepreneurs and artists. In a cramped space next door was a young couple experimenting with a Bloody Mary mix. They would frequently come over asking us to taste the concoction. *Too much pepper? Too spicy?* Their success story is that the same tomato mix we were trying became the popular Mrs. T's—still served today worldwide and on nearly every airline.

While I was designing downtown for various companies, Jerry was decorating the room's walls with bright blue burlap we'd found in an off-price store. He painted the front door and the wall trims

Kelly green, and those two colors would become the store's identity.

Without enough money to buy ready-made merchandise, to supplement the swimsuit with other items, we started producing garments from scratch. A friend's cleaning person sewed shirts, enabling us to stock the store and pay him when they were sold.

At night, using fabrics we bought at a discount store, I cut out pants and swimsuits by hand on a makeshift table, dropping off the fresh cuts at seamstresses the following morning on my way downtown and retrieving the finished products on my way back to the store that night.

The clothing sold as fast as we could make it, and the more we sold the more we were able to produce. I kept on cutting the pants and swimwear at night until I could no longer handle the amount of work involved, at which point I found a downtown menswear contractor to cut and sew the ever-growing quantity of merchandise.

In a matter of three months, word began to get around, and the tight cotton shirts and hip-hugging pants were becoming a "have-to-have" fashion with the West Hollywood gay community. But it wasn't just gay men who were eager to buy our clothes. Beverly Hills ladies began climbing the steep stairs to shop for their unwitting husbands, exclaiming how divine it was and that it was exactly like being in a European boutique.

We created door-to-door advertising flyers with a drawing of a man wearing our swimsuit (done by a fashion illustrator friend), and at night we combed the West Hollywood streets, surreptitiously placing the flyers on car windshields. That simple sketch of the man became the AH MEN logo.

After a successful first year in business, the one room became too tiny, necessitating a move to a larger space directly across the street in what is now the West Hollywood Public Library. Somewhere near the end of that first year, Frank and I began a new chapter in our relationship as well. We kept running into one another at parties, always acting perfectly civilized towards one another, but I could tell the bond was still there and that my feelings for him, and his for me, hadn't changed. We decided to give it another shot, and I could only hope that we had both learned from the lessons of our past together.

But a zebra can't change its stripes. Even though we had a new lease on our relationship, Frank still had a wandering spirit. The difference this time was that I knew exactly what I was signing up for. Before long, he started spending more time at his 54th Street apartment in Manhattan, and word would get back to me about a new boyfriend or his cavorting with hustlers at Rounds, a well-known pick-up bar. However, when he returned to LA, we would always kiss upon meeting, hold hands when alone, and know it was us. Just us. And, for the most part, I was good with that.

I, too, had several open affairs, introducing Frank to a few but never discussing the details. During one of our telephone calls, he said, "Larry, I wish you would name them all Ronnie because I can never remember which is which." He never mentioned his peccadillos to me, either, or if there was ever a serious affair, I never acknowledged it. I figured it was better not to say anything than to make it seem more important than it was. Frank enjoyed afternoon lovemaking with hustlers, his rationale being if he "did it" in the afternoon then it left the evenings free for socializing and not having to think about sex.

At work, additional funds were needed to pay for the expansion and stock the larger store, and in 1961, a corporation was created with more friends investing and becoming stockholders.

My design career started demanding more of my time. I was forced to scale back at the store to only help find more contractors as it continued growing and to occasionally assist at the biannual all-night sales. Finally, I bowed out completely, assuming a role as a major stockholder but no longer working for the company in any capacity. From the profit of that changeover, and with the encouragement of Frank, I was able to pay for my first trip to Europe.

FOURTEEN

J'aime Paris

With my AH MEN money and a check Frank gave me, I embarked on another life-changing event—as Frank called it, "The college education I never had." Europe had been on my agenda since I was a young kid, and now that I had the chance to finally experience it, I was determined to see as much as I could during my three-week visit.

After visiting London, Madrid, Rome, Venice, and Florence, Paris was the last city on my trip.

The train from Florence to Paris, with a stop in Milan, took over thirteen hours. After boarding, I wandered from car to car, taking the first empty one I found and curling up on two seats to sleep. The journey was made less tiresome, however, when a charming Italian man arrived midway through and wanted to talk. We chatted for the rest of the trip and, when we parted in Paris, he gave me his card and told me to call him for a drink sometime. I put the card in my pocket and didn't think more of it.

Tired but excited to be in Paris, l checked into the very inexpensive Left Bank Hotel Crystal where I'd heard artists, musicians, and gay people stayed. The hotel was so cheap and so bare-bones bones there was only electricity at night and hot water during the day. I dropped my bags in the tiny room, washed my face, and sauntered up the street to the iconic open-air Café de Flore (the terrace is now covered, but in those days the terrace was completely open to the street).

The maître d' seated me at the last available empty table, and I promptly ordered (in my well-rehearsed French) a *Kir*, a drink I'd read savvy French people drank. I was so delighted to be in Paris at last and loved simply taking in the sights and sounds from that seat. At a nearby table, I overheard a woman saying in English to her friend this was the first warm night of the year, and that there was a full moon. I turned around and before I looked up to try and find the moon, I looked over at the woman speaking and realized she was the famous actress Simone Signoret, and she was holding hands with the American actor Stuart Whitman. I thought, "Wow, now *this* is Paris! Wait till the folks back home hear about this!"

As I sat there sipping my drink, I was approached by a young American guy asking if he might join me since he saw I was alone and there were no other tables available on the terrace. I nodded yes, and as soon as he sat down, he began telling me with a big grin on his face that he was on his first European trip, had just graduated from Harvard, and wasn't this all just so wonderful? Enthralled and preoccupied looking at my surroundings, I barely spoke (or listened), simply nodding and saying "yes, yes" to his remarks. Finally, he looked at me and said, "You speak very good English." I laughed and said, "I should. I just arrived an hour ago." We then chatted about our dreams of coming to Paris and decided we would tour the city together. However, after a couple of days, when I told him I was gay, our connection suddenly got severed and I never saw him again.

The gay nightlife in Paris was centered on the Left Bank, specifically in the quarter of St. Germain. The bars I frequented were Le Nuage, a small room holding only fifty patrons, and down the street on the Rue du Cherche-Midi, Le Fiacre, which had a restaurant on the upper floor often filled with celebrities and a very crowded and smoky bar on the main floor. The bars Le Cherry Lane and Le Prelude were for men, and Le Monocle catered to lesbians. On the corner of Boulevard St. Germain and Rue de Rennes was the newly opened Drugstore, a 24-hour pharmacy modeled after American drugstores with a simple café on the second floor. At night, in front of the Drugstore stood many young good-looking male hustlers waiting to be picked up. Years later, I found out that two of my now-close friends had both been gigolos on that corner. C'est la vie!

It was at Le Nuage that I met the fascinating Paris celebrity Manouche. Hearing me order a drink with my heavy American accent, she turned and said in a deep whiskey voice, "Oh, you are American." When I confirmed that I was, she took a deep drag off her cigarette and then asked if I knew her "silly boy" Jean-Paul who lived in New York. I told her I lived in California and that I did not know her son. At that, she downed her drink, ordered another, and walked away. In later years, I would eventually meet her son Jean-Paul (he was also in the fashion business), and we ultimately became friends. Jean-Paul explained who his mother was and how difficult it had been growing up with her. Manouche had been the mistress of the don of the Corsican Mafia and a cabaret singer famed for her vulgarity. The French loved her.

On the more circumspect Right Bank, across the street from the Palais Garnier Opera House, the American Express office acted as a travel agency, a money exchange, and a place where foreign travelers could pick up their mail. On the lower floor were the men's and women's toilets, the men's being where sexual activity occurred most days. Picking up my mail from the United States or changing my American Express Travelers checks into French francs, I never failed to pop into the men's room for a quickie. As they say, "When in Rome..."

American Express Travel had bus tours named American Express By Day and American Express By Night. It was a great way to get acquainted with the city and visit attractions like the Louvre, the Eiffel Tower, and Montmartre during the day, or the Moulin Rouge, Lido, Alcazar, and other clubs at night. Paris is a walking city, and I walked from early morning until late afternoon every day taking in the sights, strolling in the Tuileries and along the Seine, browsing the numerous kiosks selling vintage magazines and used books, and just breathing in the beauty of the city. Although I didn't speak French, I tried to blend in and wear my American clothing in a French manner. American men wore their jeans around their hips while the French guys had them pulled tight on the waist with a discreet belt. There were other subtle elements I tried to emulate and did it so well that tourists, assuming I was French, would ask me for directions. One rule I learned was: No white socks!

Before I'd left for Europe, Frank had written to a friend of his, John Taylor, an American who had lived in Paris for many years and was awarded the prestigious Croix de Guerre by the French government for his underground work during World War II. The letter informed John of my upcoming visit and suggested perhaps he and I could meet. Upon returning to my hotel one afternoon, there was a message inviting me to a cocktail party John was hosting at his penthouse apartment in Montparnasse.

I arrived at the party and was immediately introduced to a mix of French, American, British, and Dutch guests. One who most impressed me was a woman named Ginette Bernier, the directrice of the haute couture dress house Pierre Balmain. Another guest was the officious American socialite Jerry Zipkin, whose loud voice dominated the conversation of his group. However, I soon struck up a conversation with a man about my age, Michael Franklin, whom I learned was the boyfriend of the famous British playwright Terrence Rattigan. Toward the end of the party, John invited me to join a small group of men going to a restaurant a bit later. Rattigan's lover smiled and said he was going, then coyly suggested we should go with the group of eight and continue our conversation.

Three taxis were called and off we went to La Rose de France on the Île de la Cité, a charming restaurant on a small street on an island in the middle of the Seine. Jerry Zipkin, practically shouting at his elderly and somewhat deaf dinner partner, regaled him with stories about Queen Marie of Romania. "Oh, my dear. Those rubies, *those rubies*!" he yelled. "Her jewels were *magnificent*!" Michael and I sat saying nothing but rolled our eyes, trying not to laugh. The ridiculousness and superficiality of the whole conversation nearly put us on the floor.

After dinner, John invited me back to the apartment for a nightcap, and shortly after we got there, he said goodnight and went to bed. That left me alone with Michael, who suggested we go out on the rooftop terrace and have our drinks there. As we stood high above the city, he grabbed me and began kissing me; then, right there on the roof, we began to make love. Our lovemaking became more and more passionate and, at one point, as we rolled near the edge of the terrace, I looked down and my fear of heights kicked in and I fainted. For years after that, Michael regaled crowds and dinner parties with the story, saying that he was such an exciting lover that I passed out after climaxing. The story became a legend among our mutual friends.

A French friend whom I had known when he lived in Los Angeles had moved back to Paris and was now the manager of the bar Le Fiacre. The small bar was always crowded and one evening a man came up to me and he introduced himself as Jean de Rohan-Chabot (a royal name that meant nothing to me at the time) and said he was a friend of Frank's. We chatted for a while until a friend of his joined our conversation and suggested he and I leave the noisy bar together to go to his apartment where we could talk comfortably over a quiet drink.

In the taxi, he chatted with me in precise British English, asking about my first visit to France. We arrived on Avenue Montaigne in the posh Eighth Arrondissement and entered an apartment building directly next to the famous Christian Dior offices and boutique. The apartment was decorated in authentic *Louis Louis Louis* (what we jokingly called an excess of Louis XVI antiques) and my host suggested I relax while he prepared our drinks. I asked if I might take a bath because the bar had been so warm and crowded and I was feeling sweaty. He showed me into an opulent rust-colored marble bathroom and filled the tub for me. I luxuriated in the large tub for longer than expected, and my host finally opened the door to inquire if I was okay. He looked down at me with a shocked expression and, at the same moment, I too looked down at the water. It was filthy; I hadn't bathed in a couple of days due to the lack of hot water in my hotel. After an unsuccessful bout of lovemaking, I left his apartment at 4 a.m. On the largely deserted street, trucks were going by with soldiers holding weapons because there had been a rash of bombings in Paris protesting the Algerian War.

When I left Paris, I was smitten, and I vowed to return as soon as possible. I've made good on that vow, visiting the City of Lights every year since 1961, an annual ritual going on sixty-two years.

FIFTEEN

A Tragedy

I returned to Los Angeles to find the AH MEN store and Jerry's ideas booming. He was creating jumpsuits, bathrobes, sexy underwear, and a facial products line for men that were all instant successes.

Unable to handle it alone, Jerry had hired a sales assistant but found himself needing someone with more business acumen, so he hired a bartender friend, Don Cook, to manage the new store. Don always seemed to live comfortably on whatever amount of money was available to him, and when we first met, he was living solely on unemployment funds. Whenever I visited his apartment, I noted the refrigerator was always full, and that was a good enough recommendation for me to hire him to run the store's finances. Although not creative, he was a great match for the very creative Jerry.

After a few more years of increasing success, an even larger and more visible shop was needed, so Jerry and Don relocated to the highly trafficked Santa Monica Boulevard. They published a direct mail catalog featuring photographs of scantily dressed male models wearing Jerry's exclusive designs. The mailing list was a compilation of every category of customer with addresses in all fifty states. (When my father died at age seventy-three, I found a copy of the catalog in his bureau drawer.) The catalog became red hot because until then, nobody had so brazenly and openly shown photographs of sexy clothing on almost naked models like those in the titillating AH MEN pages.

With the success of the store, Jerry began associating with people whom I repeatedly warned him were "wannabes and hangers-on." He started hosting expensive parties, inviting those who fed his ego, and used company money to pay for the soirées, constantly claiming they were good publicity for the business. We had numerous arguments regarding the measurable value of those parties, but my advice fell on deaf ears.

What Jerry refused to understand was that the store was no longer his private domain but a corporation with stockholders to report to. After a while, hearing of his spending, one of those stockholders demanded a meeting. The idea was not to attack Jerry but to listen to his reasons for spending company money on entertainment.

On the evening of the meeting, a small group of us sat in the closed Santa Monica Boulevard store casually asking questions about the use of the money and its impact on revenues. The stockholder who'd asked for the meeting was visibly angry, but the rest of us tried to keep the conversation as calm as possible. Jerry, obviously nervous, wasn't very convincing in his responses, prompting a vote to determine if, going forward, he would be accountable for any further monies spent outside of the operations of the store. The proposition was met with a resounding "yes" by the board, and in the end, Jerry agreed to the resolution and terms. At that, there was a collective sigh of relief and we all shook hands.

After everyone had left, Jerry, Don, and I went to a restaurant for dinner, where nothing of the previous discussion came up. Jerry seemed to be in good spirits, but I still sensed a bit of tension in the air.

Early the next morning, a friend called with awful news. He lived in an apartment in the same building as Jerry, and at 8 a.m. had entered the garage and smelled an odor seemingly coming from Jerry's car, which was parked next to his. He noticed the locked car's motor was running, and that's when he walked up to the driver's side door and saw Jerry slumped over the steering wheel.

Jerry's neighbor immediately called the police and waited for the ambulance and fire department to arrive. The first responders broke through Jerry's car window but unfortunately, it was already too late; he was pronounced dead at the scene, asphyxiated by deadly fumes.

It was a sad time. My best friend was gone, and I'd been so shocked by it all that the suddenness of the loss would take a long time to work through.

The stockholders were notified, and, without Jerry's energy and innovative talent, they began to lose interest in the store, offering their shares for sale. One by one Don began buying them out, finally acquiring all the shares except mine, which I decided to keep for sentimental reasons. After a year or two, I finally agreed to sell, giving full ownership to Don. Surprised by my action, he asked me why I was selling. I simply said, "I only did it for Jerry." What I meant by that was that we'd been lovers when it all began, and I still had a deep feeling in my heart for him; we'd become loving friends over time. I knew it was a great idea when he'd first mentioned it and I knew that I could help him. The timing was great, and so I went for it. I extended myself because it was the natural thing to do. And I'd have done it all over again for Jerry. He was a terrific friend, just a sweet and simple kid from Oklahoma who unfortunately got swept up in the allure of Hollywood and couldn't get out from behind it when he needed to the most.

Think Pink: A Life In Fashion

In the fashion industry, you are only as good as your last collection. Sometimes mine were not so good and I'd get fired for not meeting sales expectations. I worked for a variety of dress manufacturers, never designing under my name but under the name of the company, so at least the less successful designs didn't have my name on them forever, which would help me out if I did start designing things under my name.

The characters who owned the companies I worked for were fascinating. Hardly anyone had been to college, almost no one was particularly cultured, and many of them were first-generation Americans who had pulled themselves up to achieve the American Dream, working hard and becoming successful and rich clothing manufacturers.

Vera Horowitz was a domineering boss with a milquetoast husband. Each morning when I arrived, she would scream across the room, "LARRY!" Without fail, it would startle me so much that the coffee would jump out of the paper cup in my hand. Then, there was the old Russian boss at De Michel. He was so cheap he required I hand in my pencil stubs before I was issued new pencils. I have no idea what he planned to do with them; I suspect it was about control more than anything. When the buyers bought dresses with pleats, they would count them, knowing when he delivered the final product he might cheat on fabric and produce a dress with fewer pleats than originally shown.

One Christmas, another tight-fisted boss gave me a small frozen chicken instead of a gift or bonus, so I waited until I was the last person in the office and left the frozen bird on his desk, knowing it would be three days before he returned. At yet another company, I designed sweaters with crochet trim. There were thirty women in the factory busily crocheting, and I loved to walk in on them and say loudly, "I don't hear those needles clicking!" Which always made the ladies laugh.

Not every manufacturer was eccentric; I did work for a few who were absolute delights. A pioneer in California fashion, Pat Premo, was one of them. Pat, the designer, and her husband, Herbert Schminke, who managed the company, lived in a large house on Sunset Boulevard in Beverly Hills. They were among the few cultured persons I'd ever worked for.

Then there was Eve Bonsall. All about Eve. The Bonsall family were early settlers in California. Shul Bonsall was a descendant, and he and his wife Eve lived with their children in a traditional brick house in swanky Hancock Park. I was introduced to them by a man who told me they were looking for a designer for a new company they were opening. I would create the image of the label, Miss Eve. Eve was bored. She had always adored fashion and thought having a dress company would keep her occupied and sufficiently stimulated. The Bonsalls were lovely people, and the idea of creating a completely new company was intriguing.

I readily accepted the position as head designer. The collections I created were well received by the best stores in America, and things were going along swimmingly until I realized the man running the company was a con artist and had no experience in the industry. After finishing one of the collections, I took a week's vacation and, upon returning, he declared he'd hired his boyfriend as the new lead designer, and I was fired. But I had a contract, so I contacted my lawyer, sued, and won. The Bonsalls couldn't have cared less about the lawsuit. They'd started the business because they were wealthy and had the means to do so. The company soon closed, but during the time I worked there the Bonsalls had introduced me to many of their friends, and although we were no longer professionally involved, the Bonsalls and I remained friends.

Overall, I worked in the industry designing dresses for thirteen years. It was exciting, frustrating, and emotionally draining. Despite not having had the foundation that comes from working as an assistant, I did get continuous on-the-job training and never stopped learning throughout my career. My reputation in the dress market was solid and my designs were sold in the best stores in America. One time, my dresses were in all the windows in Neiman Marcus Dallas for an early spring collection—linen dresses with a big applique cartoon animal on each one. Success in the design world felt great, and I never felt overlooked. Most of the world only ever knows a handful of designers, but those big names are a tiny percentage of the total number of designers in an enormous industry. Every time one of my designs sold well or got covered in the press, it felt great and motivated me to keep going. Of course, you can't win all the time in fashion, and, as the saying goes, what's hot one day is not the next. Once, a friend and I were browsing the dress racks in a Goodwill used clothing store and I spotted one of my designs—a green chiffon dress—and screamed, "BILLY! Here is one of my dresses!" Every woman's head in the place did a double take. Nobody ever wants to see their work in a secondhand store, but by then I was transitioning out of my dress career and was able to have a good laugh about it.

By 1968, the women's clothing field had changed. People without a formal design education were creating innovative and exciting clothes. In London, those clothes were part of the "Mod" period (an abbreviation of modern). A newly opened boutique on Fairfax Avenue displayed wonderful little dresses in the window and I would pass the store in the evening looking at the dresses and wishing I could design like that. I called them "bag of bones, hank of hair" dresses. They were simple in shape, made with either chiffon or crepe, and ingeniously appliquéd and trimmed with bits of flowers, yarn, or whatever seemed to be at hand. Somehow, these dresses were individually beautiful and created by free spirits, inspiring a new fashion.

Many designers like me were highly trained in the style of the French designer Balenciaga, which meant simple design, beautiful fabrics, and solid construction. We studied how a garment was created for the best visual effect and how the construction had been devised. A perfect example of this is the Pyramid dress by Yves Saint Laurent, which looked effortlessly created. However, to maintain the shape, the inner lining was highly constructed with bone stays. This construction allowed the dress to maintain the rigid pyramid silhouette on a hanger—or the woman wearing it.

For hours, we established designers would discuss our opinions of how a collar should "roll" or how to "set" a sleeve, but it was obvious to us these new creators didn't give a damn about all that, and the fact remained that their dresses were selling and ours were not. Many traditionally trained designers could not understand the new style or figure out how to replicate it. Some designers were either fired from their jobs or gave up trying to emulate Mod fashion and dropped out of the field completely. Luckily for me, as I was scrambling to figure out what to do next, along came another fortuitous phone call with another perfectly timed opportunity.

Taking a break at my sister Sandy's Tehachapi ranch.
From the author's collection.

SIXTEEN

Mike Bain (The Store)

Unbeknownst to my old friend Michael Bain, he saved me just as my career as a dress designer was failing. Designing clothes had prepared me for the next phase of my life: my entry into the field of menswear.

Michael and his wife Kay were friends of mine, and they had a lot of money to spend. Michael liked wearing beautiful clothing and decided he wanted to open a men's clothing store. It seemed like a good idea, but he had no clue how to do it nor any knowledge of the retail business. Over dinner one evening, he and my sister discussed his idea, and she reminded him that I'd launched the store AH MEN, plus I had retail experience and excellent taste in clothing. Hence, a call from Michael the following day asking me to help. Would I be a part-time buyer for the store?

I quickly realized this was an opportunity for me to escape my sinking dress career and said no, not part-time. I wanted to be a full partner and the buyer. After a brief discussion, he agreed, and at that moment I embarked on a new career in menswear design and retail.

Of course, I had no idea how to buy clothing for a store or set up a budget, but I did have connections all over the industry. I called Arthur Englander, the merchandise manager friend at Neiman Marcus in Dallas, who recommended a company in Los Angeles that assisted in budgeting based on buying and selling volume. The night before my first buying trip to Europe, another friend who'd been a buyer at the prestigious I. Magnin stores explained sizing and quantity ordering. That was all it took. I was off and running.

At the first showroom I went to, I met with a salesman representing several European collections.

"You're wearing a Brooks Brothers suit," he said coldly, "what are you doing buying high-end trendy European merchandise?"

"I am just buying this shit," I said. "I don't have to wear it."

I learned a lesson on that trip though, which was that I could always be "selling" if I wore the designs I was buying. So, from then on, I was transformed. I began to wear the latest European fashion, albeit keeping it simple and classic. Contrary to the baggy Brooks Brothers look, the clothing fit more tightly, showing off my trim and fit physique. I still recall that my chest size was a size 36 inches and waist 28 inches.

Michael rented two spaces in a Sunset Boulevard mini-mall, and the interior designer Ron Wilson broke down the dividing wall, creating a large room with an adjoining tailor shop and office. He designed a comfortable and inviting store using warm wood and leather furniture. Clothing, if not hanging, was folded on easily accessible tables, and PEPI, a jewelry collection recognized by the cognoscenti, had its own free-standing counter. As I mentioned previously, the store was in a great location and soon became popular with celebrities ranging from Elvis to John Lennon and Diana Ross.

On my European buying trips, with my design background and brief retail history, I was able to speak the industry language of the designers and manufacturers in Europe. If I had an idea for a sweater, I would go to the Italian manufacturer, explain the idea, and after lunch, the knitted sample would be ready for me to see. There were many "firsts" in the designs as well. At that time, men's cashmere sweaters were two-ply knit in either a 1 ½" round or V-neck. I had sweaters made with single ply, the same weight as a cotton T-shirt— with a ½"-band on the round neck. The Italian manufacturer balked at first, stating cashmere was "*classico*," but I held my ground and got what I wanted. I called it the "cashmere T-shirt." Today, many manufacturers produce one-ply cashmere sweaters, but at the time, this was novel in the industry. To this day, if I run into a former customer, I get compliments on the originality of my clothes, and some people even still wear them.

I worked six days a week in the store, putting in long hours, arriving before it opened, and staying after it closed. Michael Bain treated it as an expensive hobby, and an increasing coke habit was steadily changing his personality. If he accompanied me on buying trips, he'd insist on bringing a girlfriend. After six years and just before I left on one of those trips, he suggested his current girlfriend Barbara should come with me to the European collections to help with the buying. I had just tried for the second time to quit smoking and was still quite agitated and going through withdrawal, and his comment didn't sit well with me at all. My growing frustration with his laissez-faire attitude and his often-drugged state finally pushed me over the edge, and I exclaimed, "If you want your girlfriend to be the buyer, then you can buy me out!"

Boom! Negotiations between lawyers began that week, and I left to embark on another escapade.

SEVENTEEN

You Are A Living Legend

Barry Bordofsky, a dead ringer for Olympic swimmer Mark Spitz, and I had been involved in an affair for a few years. He was lovable and kind, and even Frank adored him. Barry was a salesman at Jerry Magnin, a high-end men's clothing store on Rodeo Drive. When I left Mike Bain, I discussed an idea I had with him to open an office in Paris where I could serve as a liaison between American men's store buyers and French manufacturers. Not only did he think it would work but he said he would love to come with me to Paris.

During my six years as a buyer, I gained a respectable reputation in the marketplace and met and socialized with designers, manufacturers, and the owners of the finest men's clothing stores on our mutual buying trips in the European capitals. Even old Barney Pressman, the owner of the famed high-end New York department store Barney's, came up to me one day in Paris and said in his heavy European accent, "Mr. Chrysler, you are a living legend!" It was quite the compliment from a man of his stature, and with praise like that, I felt confident that my idea would be a success.

I contacted fifteen of the best men's clothing stores in America and they all agreed to be my clients, which would include paying me a commission on all orders placed. On our way to France, Barry and I visited stores I'd never seen to familiarize ourselves with their image and customers' tastes. Ultimo in Chicago, Weinstein's in New Orleans, and a few others around the country.

When we arrived in Paris, I lunched with my former Buying Office representative, a woman with whom I'd always had a warm relationship. I told her about the office I was opening, and she was delighted and said since I was now to be on their side of the business, she'd make me aware of the idiosyncrasies of my clients. That information prepared me for what turned out to be an arduous and ultimately unfulfilling experience.

Barry and I subleased an apartment in the Sixteenth Arrondissement and, with a friend's contacts, hired gorgeous young women to work the first season as interpreters assisting the buyers. The evening before the collections began, we gave a cocktail party introducing everyone to their respective translator and handed out the buying appointment schedules of the new and exciting designers and their showroom addresses.

When I visited the manufacturers, I faked it again, hemming and hawing in my limited French, but I somehow managed to get the business rolling. The buyers were happy with the new collections I proposed, and soon they began placing orders. Getting them to pay me, however, was another story, and it took a lot of long-distance phone badgering to finally get the commission checks in the mail.

When the second season rolled around, we went through the whole process a bit more efficiently, having learned a lot during our first year. But this time, after the clients left, I received a telephone call from a manufacturer who said there was a credit problem with one of the stores and that they were holding the merchandise until it was resolved. Unbeknownst to me, some of the stores were not divulging the number of orders they'd placed, thereby not paying me my commission. My job was to be certain their orders were shipped on time, and I was shocked these supposedly trusted owners and buyers would be so sneaky.

One store owner blatantly (and brazenly) told me that since they knew the addresses of the showrooms and manufacturers there wouldn't be any further need for me. I was hurt by people's dishonesty and lack of integrity but pursuing payment any further proved to be futile. Having lost my faith in their ethics and running low on funds, I faced the fact that the venture hadn't worked.

I had no idea what I would do next, so just before leaving Paris I went to the office of Maurice Biederman, the owner of Pierre Cardin clothing and Saint Laurent shirts. Maurice and I had a warm working relationship, and I hoped maybe he'd have an opportunity in mind for me. Even though I didn't buy from any of his companies, he'd often pick me up in his chauffeured Rolls-Royce where we'd get driven to a party at his sister Regine's nightclub. I'd lost faith in many other people in the fashion world at that point, but I knew I could be completely honest with Maurice about my dilemma. After pouring my heart out to him, he said whatever idea I came up with he would back me financially. With that assurance, we left Paris, but I still had no idea what I would do. I was worn out and exhausted having put my heart into the Paris office. So, it was a Catch-22: on the one hand, I had a blank canvas and an incredibly generous financial offer; on the other hand, I had no idea what on earth to do with it.

Back in Los Angeles, Barry was able to get his old job back, and we renewed our social life. The early '70s were a gay sexual free-for-all. In 1977, Barry and I were invited to the fortieth birthday party of a well-known English contemporary artist hosted by the gallery owner who represented him, at his prestigious gallery on Santa Monica Boulevard in West Hollywood. The theme was "Come As Your Favorite Fantasy," and we were asked to dress up accordingly. Barry and I both dressed as our retail idol, Gerry Stutz, the director of the New York boutique department store Henri Bendel. We wore blue blazers, silk shirts, pearls, turbans, and short wraparound skirts, and we looked, to put it modestly, lovely.

The gallery windows facing the busy street had been covered with brown paper, so the interior was hidden from view. Inside, the walls had been stripped bare of all paintings. We were immediately confronted with the smell of poppers and marijuana. Many guys were dressed up as Marines and others were in a variety of body-revealing costumes, and everyone was dancing to the blaring sound of disco music. About thirty minutes after we'd arrived, the DJ lowered the music and everyone stopped dancing, then turned to watch as two men dressed in black leather pants, jackets, and boots held open the front door to reveal a large cardboard wall joining the party assisted by two similarly dressed men. The wall was painted with graffiti and adorned with large round openings. The man inside the wall then lowered himself to the floor and mashed his face against one of the openings, servicing a horny, drunk, and stoned guest as we all looked on. The crowd went wild, and immediately a frenzy of men started unzipping their pants and pushing their penises into the holes in the wall, awaiting their turn. The party was on!

More primly dressed, Barry and I made our way through the crowd to the rear of the room, where we were soon accosted by a group of rowdy guys who pulled off our skirts and turbans, leaving us partially naked and exposed, wearing only our shirts, navy blue blazers, socks, and shoes.

The party grew even wilder and more bacchanalian as the night wore on, with many of the guests participating in all types of sexual activity. At the end of the evening, I realized I was drunk and had lost Barry in the crowd. I wandered into a room at the rear of the gallery searching for him and there was Barry, lying on a large painting, being serviced by a guest. Drunk and weaving with my hands on my hips, I yelled, "Barry! Get off that painting. You are going to ruin it!" It was five o'clock in the morning when we staggered half-naked out of the gallery, laughing as we drunkenly ran to our nearby car.

Many years later I ran into the artist at the airport in Paris and mentioned having attended his fortieth birthday bash. He said it was the wildest party he'd ever attended and would never forget it. Neither have I.

EIGHTEEN

Another Opening, Another Show

Throughout my life, inexplicable occurrences have enriched me, and I've always attributed them to those angels on my shoulders from when I was a teenager in Minneapolis. Over time, and as more serendipitous and profound events took place, I started to believe more and more in those angels as a kind of guiding force in my life. What was once just a strange encounter on a street corner became an organizing principle, a belief system even. In other words, my angels became real to me. Two instances were meeting Frank Tack and then the out-of-the-blue phone call from Michael Bain, which enabled me to change careers.

Now there was another one.

Back from Paris in 1976, I still had no idea where my retail career was heading. I was sitting in my living room watching a light spring rain patter against the outside patio, having a scotch and in a bit of a funk, when the phone rang. It was Herb Fink, the well-respected owner of seven women's clothing stores. We knew one another slightly and there was always a certain humor and mutual admiration between us whenever we met. He said he'd been sitting next to an Italian sweater representative on a plane coming back to LA from Italy when the man asked if Herb had heard I had left Paris. With that information, Herb called me as soon as he landed. He said he'd always admired my taste and had an empty retail space next to Theodore, his women's store on Rodeo Drive in Beverly Hills. Then he asked if I would like to open a men's clothing store with him.

Would I? Would I ever! Saved again!

In Theodore, all the decor was white. The salesgirls dressed in white pants, T-shirts, and sneakers, and we wanted to replicate that image in the men's store, which we named Theodore Man.

During the planning stages, Herb and I met frequently at his Malibu rental house to discuss ideas. One day, Barry happened to be there along with Herb's wife, Norma, and they were sitting at the other end of the room chatting away. At one point, I overheard Norma tell Barry she just couldn't seem to get close to me, to which Barry replied, "Don't."

His advice was prescient.

On my first buying trip to Italy for Theodore Man, I was asked by the Basile international sales representative who was backing me. That was when I found out that both Herb's and especially Norma's reputations were not exemplary, to say the least.

"I don't want that man in my showroom," the rep said, and I assured him it was only me doing the buying for the store, not Herb and Norma.

Sarah, our buying agent in Europe, represented both Herb and me on our respective buying trips. She once told me Herb and Norma had a stormy relationship, often resulting in lethal swearing arguments in public places. Norma had opened her own sportswear company and would accompany Herb to Europe to view collections, then return to LA and "adapt" what she'd seen for her collection. At the Versace collection, as usual, they were seated in the front row because the store on Rodeo Drive was considered an important showcase for the firm. In Paris and Milan, there are always young male ushers observing the audience at a showing to make sure no one is photographing. At Versace, Norma was angry with Herb—as she often was about one thing or another—and fed up with her haranguing, he signaled to one of the ushers and whispered, "This woman next to me is a designer and she is sketching." At that, the man took Norma by the arm and escorted her out onto the street.

When Theodore Man was about ready to open and the salesmen were still arranging the stock, a ladder was used to prop the front door open. One day, the ladder was pushed aside, and in walked an anxious man demanding to buy the jacket in the window. I explained we weren't open yet, but seeing how determined he was, I called the next-door women's store and said, "Send over money! We're in business!"

And so it began. The following morning, as I drove into Beverly Hills, I thought about how far I'd come. A poor Jewish kid who grew up in the projects in the Midwest, and now here I was with a store on the fabled Rodeo Drive. I had traveled a long way, indeed.

It was Broadway, baby, Broadway. I had made the big time!

From day one, the store was a smash hit. The only problem was Norma. For some reason, she had told our European agent she was out to get me, and the agent called me from Italy to warn me, imploring me to keep a low profile if I wanted to make it work. When I hung up the phone, I thought: *Who, me? Keep a low profile with a Jewish nose like this?* Then there was the "cock of the walk" business partner issue. Although Herb said he wasn't going to be involved in the men's store, he started poking his nose around at every possible opportunity, even once going so far as to order sweaters from Italy. Not only did they not sell, but one was given as a gift to a well-known singer, and it was so ugly she returned it. When I confronted him, he said, "Don't worry, we'll write it off as publicity."

I stared at him, completely dumbfounded. "Publicity?"

"All press is good press. It's publicity because everyone is talking about how ugly they are."

He had me there. I had no choice but to laugh.

Despite our missteps and Herb's increasingly heavy hand, the store continued to flourish, which was great for my professional life but not so great when it came to my personal life. Even though I'd mentioned the store to Frank on numerous occasions and told him how proud I was of it, he never once asked me how it was going or expressed any interest in visiting me there. And Mother's health continued to decline. She'd gone into a nursing home in 1973, and no matter how busy things got with work, I would make time to go see her in Santa Monica as often as I could.

My sister Judy was living up in northern California, Sandy was on her ranch in Tehachapi, California, and Dad wasn't well—plus he and I rarely spoke to one another. It was left up to me to look after Mom, which I gladly did, but after a while, it started to take its toll. I had a lot of pressures on me in all directions, off and on tension with Frank, the everyday stress and financial pressures of running a business, and Mom's deteriorating health. Sometimes when I look back and think about it, I have no idea how I could pull it all off and show up for everything demanding my time.

When I had the office in Paris, Jerry Magnin was the only one of my fifteen clients who worked like a professional. Most of the others were "bumping into walls." Jerry's store on Rodeo Drive, with his name emblazoned on the sign adjoining his Polo Ralph Lauren shop, was just down the street from Theodore Man. Aside from Herb, Jerry had been the other person I spoke to upon my return from Paris, and I'd suggested since we had had a good working relationship that perhaps I could join him in his store someday. Unfortunately, he didn't currently have an opening.

Frank Mascarelli, one of Jerry Magnin's employees told me Jerry didn't want to speak to me because he was upset that I'd opened the store. I called him to tell him what I'd heard, and he said: "You opened on my street!" I reminded him I'd offered to join him and that he'd refused.

"There was no room at the time," he said defensively, and then abruptly ended the call.

During the next couple of years, even if we saw one another at a social event, he refused to speak to me. His customers and even some of his salespeople wanting trendy sportswear were shopping at my store, not his, so I suspected he got a little bit jealous of our success.

Then one day, Jerry's secretary called, saying that Jerry wanted to invite me to dinner at the restaurant Chianti. I accepted the invitation, and when I walked in, I told the maître d', whose wife was also in the fashion business, that it was a secret I was there. Jerry was already seated when I arrived. As I approached the booth, he stood up, put out his hand, and said, "Sit down and order a drink. My father said if you can't beat them, buy them, and I'm going to make you an offer you can't refuse."

Sure enough, he made me an offer that night that I could not refuse. Trying not to seem too enthusiastic on the spot, I said I would think about it. As soon as I got home, I told Barry that Jerry was saving me from a very destructive relationship with the Herb and Norma team. He saw it the same way and encouraged me to accept the offer.

A few days later, when I thanked Herb for the opportunity he'd given me and told him I was leaving, he declared, "You hate me!"

"No, Herb," I said. "I don't hate you. I hate your wife!"

NINETEEN

Make Me An Offer

Jerry Magnin sold nice, classic merchandise, but it wasn't unique or unusual. At the entrance to the store, there was an enormous piece of sculpture blocking the view of the interior, forcing customers to decide whether to go left or right upon entering. It almost seemed to bar the way rather than inviting them into the store. On my first day there, I had the sculpture removed. Some of the old-guard salespeople were shocked, but this was only the beginning of the transformation into an exciting "new" place to shop.

The adjacent Polo store was classic, but that wasn't my aesthetic at all. The store, Jerry Magnin, was in desperate need of a new identity, something to help it stand apart from the rest. And my vision worked. Not only was the merchandise trendy, but I even went as far as to have all the shelving painted from its original dark brown to pale cream to offset the dreary earth tones of the store.

In no time, people came in who'd never shopped there before. Some of my former customers at Mike Bain and Theodore were happy to know I was there, and the buzz got around to various important social and fashion circles.

We had our share of celebs as well, just like my other stores. Moguls like Barry Diller and David Geffen shopped on Saturdays, and Donald Sutherland frequently stopped by. The talk show host Merv Griffin and his current boyfriend dropped in on occasion, and many other, more conservative people than I'd sold to before.

In 1981, I heard that exciting fashion was coming out of Japan and Tokyo in particular. Avant-guard designers like Comme des Garçons, Issey Miyake, and Yohji Yamamoto were known worldwide, but I began to hear of new creators in Tokyo who'd not yet made their mark on the international fashion scene. Always trying to be one step ahead of the competition, I arranged for a Tokyo-based Japanese buying agent to represent the store and take me to see the collections of these up-and-coming designers.

Jet-lagged, but excited about being near the famous Ginza and exploring Tokyo, I took a taxi from the Frank Lloyd Wright-designed Hotel Imperial where I was staying to the trendy Shinjuku area to check out the shops, then returned to the hotel to walk in the Ginza, where I marveled at the enormous brightly lit neon signs and the crowds of shoppers looking in the cellphone shop windows. After dinner, with my adrenaline still pumping, I headed out to one of the two gay bars catering to foreigners.

When I walked into the Regent bar, I could have been anywhere in the world other than the Tokyo I'd seen outside. It had the same music and the same decor, but this one was mainly filled with foreigners and only a few Japanese. Some minutes later, a Japanese man came up to me and brusquely said, "I know you." He then opened his navy blue blazer and sewn on the lining was the label of the store: Jerry Magnin. He shopped in the Rodeo Drive store and had seen me there. He introduced himself as Rio Suzuki, a producer bringing Broadway shows to Tokyo. Rio and I began dating, and one evening he took me to one of the minuscule Japanese-only gay bars where I was understandably disdained as an intruder. Then, on the closing night of the musical *Ain't Misbehavin*, he invited me to a Korean barbecue restaurant. Rio, dressed in a white suit and carrying a bouquet of red roses the cast had given him and I, a foreigner, entered the restaurant where we were part of a scene out of a movie. On every table, a brazier was billowing smoke high in the air, and seeing us, the very odd couple waiting to be seated, every patron's head snapped around to stare.

The exoticism I'd experienced at night was a part of the psyche of the clothing collections I saw. Unusual color and fabric combinations and silhouettes prevailed. The only problem was sizing. Overall, the Japanese were smaller in stature than our customers and, since this was the beginning of an international market for these designers, there was a lot of back-and-forth bantering and sizing promises being made in Japanese before it was translated to me, the wary buyer. Who knew if I was being told the truth or not? I placed my orders and prayed for the best upon delivery.

On my last night in Tokyo, I went back to the foreigner-friendly Regent bar and met a young man who was half-Japanese and half-Italian. He was beautiful, and we ended up at my hotel where he spent the night. In the morning, while he was in the shower, I opened a drawer where I had hidden a 1,000 yen note only to discover it was missing. I thought, "That little shit," and looked in his pants pocket. Sure enough, there was the 1,000 yen note, which I took back. When he left, I said nothing about the money, but, as I began to dress, I took a shirt out of the drawer, and out of the folds fell my 1,000 yen note. He hadn't stolen from me after all! I could imagine him telling his friends how he'd met this nice American man who'd then stolen his money. I didn't have his phone number or address and left on a plane for California that morning. To this day I feel guilty about it, and if he happens to read this book, I will gladly return the money, with interest.

Once back at the store, I touted my new fashion discoveries. But when the anticipated delivery arrived and the boxes were all opened, it was as though we had never gone through those sizing discussions. Sweater sleeves were well above the wrist and the length barely grazed the belly button of the average American man. Pant legs hovered in what is now trendy, above-the-ankle Gen-Z fashion, but at the time was way out of vogue. Despite the sizing, there was an undeniable spark of something different in the clothing, and I continued going to Japan with other adventurous American buyers. Finally, after that first hard lesson when nothing fit, I was able to work with the other American developers and communicate more clearly to our Japanese associates how to successfully develop wearable clothing that sold out shortly after arrival in the US stores.

Dag Vesti

I was at the Pitti Uomo semi-annual menswear exhibition in Florence when a young man from Norway approached me and introduced himself as Dag Vesti. He asked if he might interview me, a Beverly Hills store buyer, for an Oslo newspaper. He explained he was a fashion design student and the local Oslo newspaper had agreed to pay his way to Florence to attend the exhibition.

At the time I met him, Dag was in his early twenties and quite attractive, enthusiastic about his love for fashion, and excited to be in Italy for the first time. I explained I had many clothing stands to visit, but if he wished to proceed with the interview, he could accompany me and have a first-hand experience of how the buying process worked. He was more than eager to join me, and the questions he asked were both interesting and insightful.

At the end of the workday, I invited him to join me and my friends for dinner that evening, whereby he admitted that his funds were extremely limited and that he had to find lodging that was within his meager budget before he could afford to go out to dinner with us. The Hotel Principe, where I was staying, had given me a very large room with two extra beds, so I offered to have him stay with me. He graciously accepted, and I reassured him it would be completely above board and that there would be no sex involved. I was pleased to make the offer because I was finally at a place in my life and in my career that allowed me to start giving back. It was only natural to do for others what had been done for me, which included lots of help and opportunities in the industry when I was first starting. Dag stayed in Florence all three days of the exhibition, and when we parted ways, we promised to stay in touch.

Occasionally, I would receive a letter telling me about school and his life. One letter informed me he was moving to New York City to attend the Fashion Institute of Technology, but first, he would like to visit me in Los Angeles. I wrote back warmly inviting him to come to stay. A few months later, he arrived in LA for a few days, and I gave him a tour of the city. He was especially taken by Hollywood, which he'd dreamt of for years. Spending more time with him, I found his innocence and enthusiasm charming, but it became clear to me that he would need a part-time job in New York to supplement his school scholarship. I suggested a knitwear designer/manufacturer I knew and told him I would call to arrange an interview as soon as he arrived in the city.

Dag was immediately hired by the designer on my commendation, and we would see each other for dinner a couple of times a year when I would visit New York on buying trips. During one dinner, he told me he frequently went out dancing at a popular gay disco named Limelight, and that he loved the energy and excitement there. I cautioned him to be careful and remember he was going to school and had a job; therefore, it was best to limit his social life to the weekends. Meanwhile, in a conversation with his boss, I was told he felt Dag was becoming involved with a shady crowd and his work had suffered. Dutch uncle that I seemed to be, I could only relate my concerns to him. He assured me he was OK and not to worry.

That conversation would prove to be an ominous but unheeded warning.

A couple of months later, I received a phone call from a New York friend asking if I knew there were posters all over Manhattan with Dag Vesti's name and physical description. He'd been missing for two weeks. A New York police department detective called soon after that, saying he had found my name and number in Dag's telephone book, and asked me a dozen questions: had I seen him recently? When was the last time I'd spoken to him? How well did I know him? How long had I known him?

Then, one dark day shortly after my conversation with the detective, the bad news arrived via a headline in *The New York Times*. Dag had been lured by his new Limelight friends to an estate in upstate New York and murdered in a sadomasochist rite. His burned body was found in an outdoor oven, and he had only been identified because a leather mask had protected his face from the flames. The murderers were arrested, but only one of them, Bernard Le Geros, was convicted of the crime. The accomplices, one of whom was Andrew Crispo, a renowned Manhattan art gallery owner, were given lighter sentences.

I often think of first meeting Dag Vesti and his innocence and enthusiasm about his future. To this day I cannot see a photograph of the type of headgear found on him without looking away in horror and disgust. Poor, sweet, susceptible Dag. I still feel that outrage whenever I think of what happened to him.

If there was any silver lining at all to come from that, maybe it's that I came to appreciate the fact that I'd always had a good internal barometer for reading people and situations. I may not have always been able to articulate why a particular person did or didn't seem trustworthy, but I was always able to steer clear of dangerous situations like the one Dag and others tragically found themselves in, which seemed to occur in greater numbers throughout the '80s.

TWENTY

I'm No Angel

As I watched more and more people self-destructing through drugs, dying from AIDS, and succumbing to depression because of all the loss around us at that time, for some reason I had the instinct to self-improve.

The job at Jerry Magnin gave me time to take longer lunch hours, which allowed me to either go to the gym or take swimming lessons from a former Olympic swimmer. I'd had a fear of drowning ever since childhood and never learned to swim, but I wanted to get over it, so I began taking lessons at a small pool. After just a few lessons, the instructor said I was strong enough to do longer laps and needed to learn in a larger pool. My partner, Frank, had bought a house with a large rectangular pool overlooking a view from downtown to Malibu, so I asked him if I could come up once a week to take my lesson. He said it was fine so long as I didn't disturb him, which I found odd given that we had been together off and on for years. I began taking my swim lessons, telling the instructor we had to be very quiet. Doing my laps one afternoon, I noticed Frank peeking out from behind the curtain, watching me swim. I knew then that despite his confusing behavior and mixed messages, he was proud of me. Not only that, but I knew that he loved me deeply and just didn't always know how to show it.

My buying trips continued taking me to Europe and New York twice a year, but even though Frank had his 54th Street apartment, I was never invited to stay there. Instead, I would book a room directly across the street at the Dorset Hotel, and if Frank was in town, I would walk across the street to meet him for a cocktail before our dinner out. There were times our relationship was so distant that it almost seemed he'd forgotten our past together. On other occasions, it was like we were dating again and nothing had ever changed from those early days.

On one of those better evenings, I met him at his apartment, and he surprised me by hiring what for him was an extravagance: a limousine to take us downtown to the newly reopened musical *Fiddler on the Roof.* It was a warm June night, and I looked spic and span in white pants, a blue Oxford cloth shirt, and penny loafers. He dismissed the limo at the theater, and after the performance, we walked to a nearby restaurant where we enjoyed drinks and dinner. Not wanting the night to end, we decided to take a taxi to a Ninth Avenue bar we'd heard about. Upon arriving, we waited in front of a warehouse for the freight elevator to take us up. Entering the crowded room, we made our way to the bar to order drinks, when I noticed a door open along a side wall to a dark room. We took a couple of bar stools, and I watched as men walked in and out of the open door into the dark room. Curiosity got the best of me, and I decided to see what was back there for myself. When I finally returned, having been gone quite a while, Frank was a bit drunk and eyeing me woefully.

"Oh, Larry," he said, like a disappointed parent.

It was obvious to both of us that we'd entered a new phase of our relationship. We were not physically intimate anymore but still enjoyed each other's company and the emotional bond that develops between two people who have shared so much history. I suppose if it had been up to me at that point, I'd rather have been with him than with men in a back room while he waited on a bar stool, but the reality was that he no longer expressed any interest in sex with me, and I'd given up trying to convince him otherwise.

At a late hour, we finally left, taxiing back to 54th Street where we kissed goodnight and saw each other off: he to his apartment and me to the hotel. As I entered, the doorman seemed to look at me oddly, but I thought nothing of it until I caught my reflection in the lobby mirror as I waited for the elevator. My shirt was soaked with sweat, I'd lost my belt, and there were footprints on my once immaculate white pants. I was no angel.

In 1983, when my mother died, Frank was in his New York apartment and called to express his condolences, asking if I planned to be in the city anytime soon. I replied I'd be there in September for one of my biannual buying trips.

"You know, Larry, I haven't given you a birthday gift in years," he said. "How would you like to go to Paris on the Concorde and stay at the Ritz Hotel for a week? You arrange the restaurants because you know Paris better than I do."

Sometimes, his generosity took my breath away. Despite Frank's many flaws, he also had an intuitive and loving way of knowing how to strike the perfect note at the perfect moment. Off to Paris we went, where we spent a week in a two-bedroom suite at the hotel. Frank's bedroom had furniture covered in peach-colored satin, intended for Madame. The living room separating the bedrooms was large, with two sofas and a fireplace. My room was more masculine, strewn with animal skins and furniture in dark, warm colors. I could have lived there forever if only I could have afforded it. At the end of the week, the bill was $8,000! (About $82,000 in 2023.)

By this time, Frank had congestive heart failure and walking had become difficult for him, so he spent much of each day resting in the suite. But without fail, at seven o'clock each evening we met in the living room for cocktails before dinner in one of my chosen restaurants. It was an unforgettable trip, and our last together.

Each time Frank returned to Los Angeles, and despite his ill health, we resumed our "dating," meeting sporadically in out-of-the-way restaurants where he was sure not to be seen in his increasingly debilitating state of illness. By this point, he was walking with a cane and had lost weight, but he still managed to keep his now wispy hair dyed black.

I didn't realize it at the time, but to cope with Frank's imminent death, I began studying piano again, having neglected it for many years. The piano was something I'd always loved, and playing was always a refuge for me. At his house one evening, while Frank was preparing our favorite dry Rob Roy cocktails, thinking I would surprise him, I went over to the piano, sat down, and began to play a Mozart sonata. He quickly came out of the kitchen and stood there with the drinks in his hands.

"Why aren't you playing Ravel?" he asked in a disparaging tone. Even after all those years, nothing had changed.

TWENTY-ONE

Those Who Make Magic

New designers began coming into the Jerry Magnin store to show me their debut collections. One was Mr. Marciano, a Frenchman, who had a small group of skinny jeans (called La Cigarette in France), which were dyed in bright glowing colors that I had only seen on women. They were unusual for men and I ordered a small number to try out. When they arrived, the legs of the jeans were so tight it was impossible to put them on. I called Mr. Marciano and he said he would remake them, which he did. When the new shipment arrived, they sold out within days. That was the prototype pant and the beginning of the company later known as Guess Jeans.

Perry Ellis had always been a womenswear designer, and when he decided to make a foray into men's fashion, he put together a small collection of men's sportswear. Only two of us buyers in the United States bought the first collection: the buyer for Henri Bendel in New York and me. To launch it, I put paper masks with a photograph of Perry's face on all eight mannequins in the store's large display windows. It was a sensational collection, and it, too, sold out within days.

Giorgio Armani was another well-known name who'd designed for three of the manufacturers I'd bought garments from. When his paramour Sergio convinced him to go out on his own with his name on the label, I was invited to see the very first collection in Milan—and was dazzled by the simple unconstructed jackets, suits in beautiful fabrics, and chic sportswear. Here was to be another exclusive "first" for me in Beverly Hills, but before he'd accept orders, he wanted to see the stores in America to be certain they were right for his image.

On my way back to California, I stopped in New York to see the Madison Avenue retailer Jackie Rogers, whom I'd met on one of my buying trips and instantly adored. Jackie's iconic New York store was a go-to destination for retailers inspired by her unique merchandise. I knew she was a friend of Armani, so I told her how much I wanted the collection and that my getting it was still in limbo. "Just a minute," she said, and picked up the phone, dialing his number in Milan.

"Giorgio, dear, it's me," she said. "Jackie Rogers." Her Boston-accented Italian sounded like she was asking a favor from the mafia. "The Jerry Magnin store has the best and biggest display windows on Rodeo Drive and is perfect for your collection." After a few more comments, she hung up the phone and said, "You got it."

A brash, no-nonsense broad, Jackie was one of the most fascinating characters I have ever met and just the type of independent woman I admired. She was allegedly described by Ralph Lauren as resembling the tough, square-jawed actor Victor Mature in drag. On one of our New York buying trips, I invited Jerry Magnin to join Jackie and me for lunch. He declined, saying he didn't think he could handle her volatile personality.

Jackie had also been raised in a poor Jewish family, which was one of the things that bonded us and forged a tight-knit, no-bullshit understanding and friendship. We both knew where we came from and had never forgotten it—and that too, helped us to appreciate how far we'd come and to hold tightly onto what we had today.

Through forceful determination, Jackie had entered a career in fashion first as a model for Coco Chanel (reputedly having been the French designer's girlfriend for a short while), then the lover of an Italian count, living with him for eight years in Bologna, and later becoming the owner of a popular men's clothing store on Madison Avenue and women's clothing stores in Southampton and Palm Beach.

She could be a crazy, spontaneous, and challenging friend; her moods often changed from minute to minute. We buyers traveled to Paris, London, Milan, Rome, Florence, Copenhagen, and Cologne searching for new ideas and merchandise, and I'd often run into Jackie in one place or another. We'd walk the exhibition halls together, dine with mutual friends, and laugh a lot.

The Messe in Cologne, Germany, exhibited men's fashion collections twice a year in enormous warehouse-type buildings with hundreds of manufacturers showcasing all categories of menswear to international buyers. One year, I ran into Jackie, who'd just arrived that morning from New York. It was now afternoon, and she claimed she'd seen nothing she liked at the show and wanted to get out of there. Hailing a cab, she pushed me in, and off we went to a bed and breakfast room she'd rented for her Cologne stay. In the room, I watched her throw a few clothes, a pair of silver high-heeled shoes, and a portable radio into her suitcase. It was as though she'd been inspired by the actress Mary Astor, who famously quipped that whenever she visited New York all she packed was a nightgown and an evening gown. We left the room and scurried out of the place, hugging goodbye, and off she went—even skipping out on the lodging bill. That was the type of unpredictability she was capable of, always living by the moment and making decisions on a whim; it never ceased to amaze me.

Pitti Uomo's exhibition in Florence showed fine quality clothing and accessories, drawing menswear buyers from the best stores in the world such as American retailers Neiman Marcus Dallas, Charivari New York, Ultimo Chicago, Jerry Magnin Beverly Hills, and Wilkes Bashford San Francisco. On one of those Florence evenings, Jackie and I were to meet for dinner at Harry's Bar, a favorite haunt of ours. Buyers would often get off a plane from the US at 7 a.m. and be working the shows by 9 a.m., jet lag be damned. However, a late afternoon nap could often turn into a complete night's sleep, ruining a planned evening out.

The evening we were to have dinner, Jackie was exhausted after a day full of viewing numerous collections, so she went back to the Hotel Excelsior to take a nap in the room she was sharing with her assistant John. Upon awakening and seeing she was running late, she groggily got dressed, grabbed what she thought was her evening bag, and then took the notoriously slow hotel elevator to the lobby. While waiting under an awning in the pouring rain for a taxi, she realized that instead of her evening bag, she had, in her haste, taken her roommate John's shave kit. She then had to go back up in the slow elevator, exchange the kit for her bag, and head back down to the lobby. Nervous about being late, she managed to get a taxi in the rain, only to rush into Harry's Bar where I had yet to arrive.

Meanwhile, in a meeting with buying agent Maureen Bonini, I glanced at my watch and realized I was late for my dinner with Jackie.

"Oh no," I said to Maureen, "I am so sorry to do this, but I'm late for dinner with Jackie."

I didn't even have to finish my sentence. Maureen knew exactly how severe Jackie's wrath could be, and she offered to drive me to the restaurant, so we jumped into Maureen's car and drove through the rain to Harry's Bar.

When we got there, the maître d' quickly walked up to me and whispered, "Be careful. Mrs. Rogers is very angry with you."

Jackie was seated at a corner table with a candle and a small flowerpot centerpiece, looking lovely in a black Chanel suit with the trademark white gardenia on the lapel. As I warily approached her table, she spotted me and yelled, "You son of a bitch!" Then she picked up the small pot and threw it at me. I ducked just in time, trying not to laugh, and set about profusely apologizing. After calming down, she proceeded to tell me of her "harrowing" evening's travails coming to meet me. I weakly explained my reason for being late, apologizing again, then kissed her cheek, flagged down the waiter, and ordered our much-needed drinks.

In the middle of one hot summer afternoon, a black limousine pulled up to the front of our menswear store, Theodore Man, on Rodeo Drive. Out stepped Jackie, clad head to foot in New York black. She walked into the store and the first words out of her mouth were, "Where the fuck are all the people? Nobody is walking on these fucking streets."

"Hey," I said, "this isn't New York, you know, this is Beverly Hills. Nobody walks here."

That incident, as much as any other, exemplifies Jackie: sometimes vulgar, independent, opinionated, and always chic with a great sense of humor.

I got to experience the softer side of Jackie during a quiet dinner we had in Milan with two of her Italian friends. That evening the conversation was mainly about family and growing up. It was then that I learned of her humble beginnings and how unhappy she had been with the noble Italian lover's prejudiced family, the jealousies she faced from the other models when she modeled for Chanel, and the strength it took to maintain enough stamina to continue working in the competitive retail atmosphere of New York City. She had offered a tough facade over the years, but this night's special and honest confession endeared her to me even more.

Jackie and I had both fought many battles to reach our level of business success. Each of us had been born into impoverished beginnings and was now at the top of our game. We never forgot where we began and always appreciated what we had become. She was recognized as a name in the retail world of New York, and I on fabled Rodeo Drive. To each of us, this was our badge of success, and perhaps it's what enabled us to understand one another and stay friends.

During another one of my buying trips, Jackie invited me to dinner along with John at Elaine's, a hangout bistro for New York's literary and society circles owned and run by the notoriously difficult Elaine Kaufman. When we entered, there sat Elaine behind the cashier's desk with her head bowed. Without so much as raising her chin an inch, she said in a disinterested voice, "Oh, hi Jackie." It was obvious there was no love lost between the two women. The three of us were led to our table by a waiter, and we proceeded to have a pleasant evening laughing, eating, and drinking our wine without giving any further thought to Elaine's mopey demeanor. Until the bill arrived.

Jackie carefully perused the bill and then called the waiter over and pointed out a charge for an extra bottle of wine we never ordered nor received.

"Isn't that right, Larry?" she said as the waiter looked at the bill. "Isn't that right, John?"

We both agreed, and, looking rather forlorn, the waiter said he would pay out of his pocket for the extra bottle instead of daring to disturb Elaine.

"Get that cunt over here," Jackie demanded.

At that, Elaine strode over to our table and pursed her lips as Jackie explained the dinner bill problem. Elaine didn't budge. If anything, she dug her heels in even further, confidently stating the bill was correct despite us (and a sheepish and now terrified waiter) insisting otherwise. That was all it took for Jackie to stand up, push her chair aside, and slap Elaine. The two women began to brawl until John, me, and the waiter forcibly separated them. Once we were outside, Jackie calmly said, "Guess it'll be a while before I go back to *that* place."

Not only did she not pay for the extra bottle of wine, but Jackie never paid for anything that night.

Two days later, the trade newspaper *Women's Wear Daily* ran a front-page article about Jackie and Elaine fighting. I called Jackie as soon as I saw it, asking her how the newspaper found out.

"It's publicity, honey, publicity," she said.

Sure enough, Jackie had called the newspaper about the evening's fracas and landed on the front page of a periodical read by nearly everyone in the fashion industry. It was free publicity, indeed, and Jackie knew as well as anyone the adage was true, "There is no such thing as bad publicity."

Swifty's was a restaurant whose main clientele was upper East Side locals, and it was one of Jackie's favorites. On another trip to New York in 2005 with my partner Matthew, I invited her to dinner there. "Of course, darling. Love it!" We walked in and she was seated at a VIP banquette looking coiffed, dressed in black, and wearing heavy Bakelite plastic bracelets on both wrists in an array of colors.

For an old dame, she looked fabulous. During dinner, couples would arrive greeting her in two distinct manners. The first were those who genuinely liked her: "Oh hi, Jackie, how are you?" The second were those whose dislike was coldly apparent: "Hello, Jackie." With Jackie, people either loved her or hated her. There was no in-between.

Now and then, Jackie would call and ask me what was happening "out there" (as Woody Allen called California), saying she was thinking of opening a store. But it never happened. Nor did the book she wanted to write. She was happy designing and dressing the women of Palm Beach and being the fabulous Jackie Rogers, but I think she was always a bit restless and looking for something new to catch her eye. To be honest, that could be said of just about everyone in the fashion business because fashion people are always looking for the next new and trendy thing.

When I heard Jackie had died at the age of ninety, all the funny stories about our relationship came flooding back. I'm sure anyone who'd had any sort of encounter with her would have felt the same.

Small store buyers fought tooth and nail to have exclusive dibs on designers in their town, but often when the designer's company grew, they began to sell to department stores as well. I tried not buying the same colors or styles as those large stores that had frequent sales, and that, too, became an ongoing battle.

For example, a typical incident would be when a man walked into the store attempting to return a shirt without a receipt. I'd turn him away, saying yes, we had the same shirt, but I would have never bought the color rust. It was obvious that he'd stolen the shirt from another store because the manufacturer and style might have been the same but not the color.

Rodeo Drive began to attract worldwide attention after the creation of the Rodeo Drive Committee's publicity storm and created a Frankenstein of sorts because we had crowds of "looky-loos" wandering into the store but never buying anything. It also brought shoplifters, and on Saturdays, I became a detective on the sales floor.

As the years went by, Jerry began to chip away at the individualism he so desperately wanted in the beginning. I had brought to the store a new image and prestige in the industry. I was receiving accolades from magazine editors, manufacturers, and other buyers, and I believe this partially contributed to his attitude, although he could be irresponsible with his comments toward me as well as the salespeople at our Saturday morning meetings.

At each Saturday meeting, I would explain the new merchandise that had been brought into the store that week, including who the designers were and what their designs projected. After my talk during one of those morning meetings, Jerry announced to the whole staff that from then on, if he tapped anyone's shoulder during the day, that meant they were fired and they were to leave the sales floor immediately. It was a sudden and deliberate blow to the enthusiasm I had just tried to instill in them.

As things got more uncomfortable and contentious with Jerry, I looked for a way to leave my position gracefully. I couldn't actively search for a new job because the industry was too personal, and at this point, I was too well-known. Word would have quickly gotten back to Jerry. The only person I held in confidence then was the owner of Merona Sportswear in New York, who also happened to be a friend, and he discreetly told me he wanted me to open a store there—but moving back to New York was out of the question.

Meanwhile, Jerry's behavior was becoming increasingly erratic and dictatorial. At one contentious meeting, he fired the store manager for disagreeing with him. Eventually, of course, it was my turn to get fired, which was inevitable at that point; I'd known for weeks that it was just a matter of time before my number was up. When I asked for a reason, he wouldn't even give me one, saying he didn't have to tell me. Despite his desire to get rid of me immediately, I refused to leave and stayed for a month to finish up the work I'd begun for the upcoming '84 Olympics.

My leaving became a big headline on the front page of the menswear newspaper, *Daily News Record*. Phone calls poured in from people in the industry claiming they always thought I was a partner and not just an associate, as Jerry had claimed.

I was initially quite peeved. After all, it never feels good to get fired, let alone from a company you helped rebuild. In time, however, I came to realize that Jerry had done me two favors: he hired me, and he fired me. His referring to me as an associate was just another one of his power moves, but it didn't take away my experience and integrity, or the truth of what I'd accomplished. That seven-year experience increased my visibility in the marketplace, and now, once again, even though I had no idea what would come next, I was free.

TWENTY-TWO

Movin' On

My mother, father, and closest friend all died during the years I worked at Jerry Magnin. With my father, I'd arranged for him to go to a nursing home on Fairfax Avenue as soon as he fell ill, but it became evident that he wasn't receiving the type of care he needed there, so I put him in the car during one of my visits and took him to a different nursing home on Olympic Boulevard. A week later, a staff member called and told me he was dying of cancer, and that they would immediately transport him to UCLA. But it was too late, and he died a couple of days after that.

When Mom died five years later, in 1983, the doctor said she was just a shell. With neither of my sisters around, I alone had to decide to "pull the plug." It was a heart-wrenching thing to have to do.

At least now that the responsibilities I'd had with both parents in nursing homes were over I could contemplate my future. Yet I'd been so busy with the store and constantly traveling on buying trips that I'm not sure I ever got a chance to properly grieve all that loss until I was unemployed again and had time to sit with my feelings and reflect on the previous few years. Jerry had told me just to come back to work the day after my father died because he thought it would make me feel better. He was only partly right. The truth was, I still had a lot of processing to do.

At the same time as I was grieving the loss of my parents, AIDS was spreading like wildfire. It was a terrifying time, especially for sexually active gay men, and the only way I knew how to cope was to channel my fears and energy into trying to help others. It was almost like a survival instinct; I had no other choice but to throw myself into trying to do something good in the face of so much bad.

At a West Hollywood gym, I put together and hosted a fundraiser I called Hot August Afternoon, soliciting donations from dozens of local clothing stores for a fashion show, and convincing two friends who were professional big animal trainers to bring a lion cub and other animals to lie around the outdoor swimming pool. I also managed to get publicity posters and beer comped, so, in the end, we had a sizable net profit. The success of this event, and the positivity it invoked in me during that dark time, encouraged me to start assisting with the newly opened thrift store Aunt Bea, later known as Out of the Closet.

Another great local charity, founded in 1989 by Marianne Williamson, was Project Angel Food, which delivered food to people suffering from serious illnesses like HIV/AIDS. I hooked up with them as well and helped coordinate a large fundraising event at the Beverly Hilton Hotel. I arranged for numerous clothing stores to donate clothing to be sold, and at the live auction on the evening of the event, I bid against the one and only Elizabeth Taylor on one of the travel packages and won. Elizabeth was a stalwart early supporter of HIV/AIDS causes and outbidding her was bittersweet.

As it turned out, the trip was one of the most memorable of my life. A friend and I flew first-class to Rome where we stayed in a five-star hotel. The first morning in Italy, we took a limousine to meet the docent of the newly renovated Sistine Chapel, where we were given a private tour of the chapel and then the Vatican art collection. The following day, we had lunch with the American ambassador to the Vatican and a private audience with Pope John Paul II. Then we took the train to Florence, where we were the guests of the conductor Zubin Mehta and his wife Nancy. After watching Mehta conduct a brilliant Maggio Musicale performance, we joined the Mehtas and a group of their close friends for dinner, where I was seated next to the famous pianist Aldo Ciccolini. If only my old piano teacher could have seen me then . . . The entire experience was nothing short of phenomenal.

I also began volunteering for AIDS Project LA, and, with their director of special events, put together an evening performance featuring my friend Bobby Short (who said celebrities usually charged for their services but that he would do it for me) and a large banquet dinner. People who'd never given a penny to an AIDS benefit bought tickets and arrived in limos; a few even became friends of mine. It was another bittersweet night: on the one hand, there were over 400 people there all in support of an incredible cause and having a great time, and yet underneath it all was the grave reality that people were still dying in droves.

AIDS was rampant, and the only thing I knew to do was to call in my "markers" and help raise money. Barry and I had split in 1978, but we still loved one another and had stayed relatively close over the years since—until he, too, became a victim of the disease and died. I then got the news that all my French friends living in Nice had died, and my first French boyfriend Jackie Lafourcade.

It was such a dark time. There's nothing new I can add that hasn't already been said about that period, but I think in the end what made it such a profound sense of loss was the fact that the crisis began so suddenly and lasted for such a long period and affected so many people that the collective sense of loss, whether you knew one person or you knew one hundred people who died, was unbearable. We were all acutely aware that for every person we lost, thousands of others were losing their loved ones, too.

But you find ways to move on. You must, otherwise you get pummeled by the weight of the grief. Despite and because of the grief, you keep going.

A Moral Victory

I had yet to find a new job when I heard there was a possibility through the Red Cross to apply to the Marine Corps for an official change of status from Undesirable Discharge to General Discharge. This would not only make me eligible for some benefits but also give me much overdue peace of mind and redress the wrong that had been done to thousands of servicemembers just like me. I immediately went to the local office and explained my case to the woman in charge. She wondered why, since I had been so successful in my career, I would want to bother with changing the discharge status. I said it was because I had never done anything sexual on base before my arrest and that it would be a moral victory to have it changed. She explained that the military decision-makers for the change of status cases were impressed by letters of recommendation written by doctors, lawyers, bankers, and otherwise notable members of the community, and she encouraged me to gather those before applying.

SCATTERSHOT

Not quite knowing how to explain my situation to the people I was going to ask for these letters, I decided to tell them I was being considered for a big job in Japan and that I needed recommendations speaking to my moral character. Why I thought of Japan, I will never know, except I did go there a few times on buying trips. Everyone I asked happily obliged. So, armed with letters from my doctor, a lawyer, and a banker, I returned to the Red Cross office and completed my application for a change of discharge status.

One year later, I received in the mail a packet containing the General Discharge, a transcript of my trial, a $25 check (for one month's pay), and an open train ticket to New York, where my original induction was to have taken place. Remembering the G.I. Bill affording free education to veterans after the Second World War, I immediately called the Veterans Administration office in West LA to find out the benefits for which I now qualified. I asked the administrator who took my call if my change in discharge status made me eligible to attend the Sorbonne in Paris, just as soldiers had been enabled to do with the GI Bill at the end of WWII.

"Honey," he replied, "I think you are a little late for that."

We both laughed, and I put the $25 check in my file, thinking, "This will fuck up their bookkeeping for at least one quarter."

I had a moral victory at last. I played the game, and I was patient, and since then I've lived to see gay rights that were once never imaginable.

TWENTY-THREE

Oh, Do It Again

Dazed by all the illness and death around me, one morning I sat down in my garden and wrote my thoughts on a yellow legal pad about the kind of work I would like to pursue next.

Not long after I sat down, boom! Up popped a new idea: open a store presenting collections by designers who designed both men's and women's clothing and establish a unique identity to the presentation of the clothing. Although I had some money, I hadn't enough to launch it on my own, so I set about brainstorming who might be interested.

Despite the popular refrain, I think most people seldom learn from their mistakes, and it seems I was chief among the "bad learners." I was a true glutton for punishment. Because who did I think would go for the idea and had the money to do it? Who was the best, most qualified person that came to mind in my time of need? Herb Fink from Theodore Man; the man whose wife Norma had been out to get me.

Of course, Herb loved the idea. His only reservation was that I'd never dealt with women in a store, and he astutely noted that their shopping habits were different from men's. I naively thought, what could be so different? Turns out, for as far as I'd come in my career, I still had plenty to learn. One thing I did differently this time around, however, was to look out for myself financially from the outset. Usually, in my retail career, the partner I'd been involved with had the money and I had the talent, but I wanted this situation to be more financially secure for me, so for this endeavor, we went fifty-fifty on our partnership. Once the sundry details were settled, we got to do the "fun" stuff, and the first order of business was deciding on the name Contents by Theodore, which we both found simple, understandable, and cool.

We decided we would put the store in the upscale shopping mall Beverly Center and flew to New York to see the newly hyped Comme des Garçon Soho store for aesthetic inspiration. We hired the highly respected architect Michael Rotondi to design the layout. In our preliminary discussion, he was quick to say how happy he was to finally work with someone who "got it." That felt good to hear, and, at the beginning anyway, the feeling was mutual. We were simpatico in our vision for the store. Or so we thought.

Herb and I wanted a clean, modern look with pale gray stone display tables and lots of white everywhere. The store had enormous windows facing the mall, which would allow passersby to see the entire interior. I'd advised Rotondi of the basic measurements and requirements I needed in designing a retail store, including hanging rods, shelves for pants, and dressing rooms. But it seems he didn't understand the creation of retail after all, because the first plans had a low-hanging ceiling at the entry which would have stopped prospective shoppers dead in their tracks. The partitions between the dressing rooms were too high, which would have exposed people to their neighbors also trying on clothes. When I confronted him about this, his reasoning was that the lines of bars in the ceiling he wanted to create carried through a line to the dressing room walls.

"This isn't the Sistine Chapel," I said. "It's a clothing store."

The arguments with Rotondi got so contentious that Herb suffered a mild heart attack, from which he fortunately recovered without too much residual damage. After that, however, I soured on Rotondi almost completely, and I told him the store would never be photographed, thereby depriving him of the publicity that would have enhanced his architectural status.

As we stocked the store for the next day's opening, we discovered the rust metal hanging rods custom-designed for the store had not been coated, and looked on in horror as flakes of rust began to dust the shoulders of the beautiful new clothing. That overlooked detail alone resulted in hundreds of dollars in dry cleaning bills each month.

Finally, opening day arrived, and the first people to enter the store were architects who'd eagerly come to see Rotunda's latest work. They were all dressed in plaid shirts with a pen in the breast pocket and corduroy pants. They sniffed around like investigators, touched the walls, and left without so much as picking up one item of clothing. When the real customers finally arrived, however, we instantly had another success on our hands.

The Ladies of Beverly Hills wandered around picking and choosing and leaving clothes on the dressing room floor, usually returning most of what they had taken so long to purchase anyway. A few weeks after our opening, Joan Rivers, dressed head to foot in Chanel, asked to have her daughter Melissa outfitted for her first year at college. The MGM swimmer Esther Williams and her husband frequently came in just to hang out before seeing whatever movie was showing at the other end of the mall. And these were just a few of the high-end clients we catered to. By all measures, we were a success—and the dreaded Norma Fink was nowhere to be seen. But there was a vibe in the store I couldn't understand, and it made me very nervous. Perhaps it was being in a closed-in mall, or perhaps, as Herb had cautioned me, it was an edginess that I felt dealing with women's different shopping habits, or maybe it was the fact that this time I had to deal with staff quitting or not showing up for work since I had more stake in the business partnership. Whatever it was, in short order, I was ready for a breakdown.

On one of the final days of our semi-annual sale, with signs all over the place (70% OFF! NO RETURNS!), the Japanese designer Issey Miyake strode in, walked straight to the back of the store where a rack had his merchandise on sale, looked at the prices, turned on his heels, and walked out. On the last day of the sale, a woman spent hours choosing so many items a salesman had to carry the over-flowing bags to her car.

At 10 a.m. the following morning, I noticed the same woman with all the previously purchased bags of merchandise standing outside of the glass front door. I opened it and she arrogantly said, "If you want to make me happy you will take all of this back!" I pointed to the NO RETURNS signs and replied, "What makes you think I want to make you happy?" At that, she threw the bags into the store and said she'd returned the merchandise and would call her credit card company to stop payment.

That did it for me. I walked into my office and called my partner Herb, saying I wanted my marbles back and that he could have the store. Sacrificing my mental health wasn't worth whatever dollar amount we were making. We dissolved our relationship shortly thereafter, and that, dear reader, was the end of my retail career. It was over for me with business partners and crazy customers.

Consulting became my next logical career move. This time, I would be on my own, and I knew there were designers needing placement and appointments with stores but with no way to get in to see the owners/buyers. My reputation was still good across the industry, and I had the contacts the designers needed. The arrangement was going well, I was consulting with everyone from a store owner ready for bankruptcy to a woman selling a custom line of cosmetics for men. Then, I had a telephone call that changed everything.

TWENTY-FOUR

Changing My Way

Frank's illness had become increasingly debilitating. One day, as we were discussing the condition of a mutual friend who was dying from AIDS, Frank very casually said, "I'm dying, too."

It happened so quickly I didn't have a chance to process the weight of it. Maybe I already knew somewhere deep inside that he was dying; he hadn't been the same Frank for months, but illness can affect a person gradually in ways that make it seem like things have always been as they are in the moment. I still couldn't stomach the thought of life without him around, though, even if we had become somewhat distant.

"You need to be back in the hospital!" I admonished him.

"No, Larry, I'm tired of all of that," he said. "When I do it, I'm not going to 'muff' it."

Given the circumstances and my spinning thoughts, I wasn't listening to the deeper implication of what he'd said. I just remember him using the word "muff," which was a jazz term meaning to flub or mess something up. That's the word I'd hear in my head over and over after he was gone. *Muff it*. And those are the words I should have paid more attention to, telling myself if only I'd heard him more clearly that day then maybe I could have done something to stop his death. But no one could have, his mind was already made up.

We continued nursing our drinks and conversing as usual, and that was the last time I'd see him alive.

The following week, I was home reading the newspaper when Frank's houseman called to tell me Frank was dead by suicide. He didn't "muff it". He did as the Hemlock Society suggested, taking Seconal sleeping pills and drinking vodka until he permanently fell asleep. Frank was gone.

Just as was his way, all his papers were precisely prepared and in order.

After his body was removed from the house, I wandered around, finding myself alone for the first time in his home office. I opened the desk drawer to find multiple bottles of sleeping pills, his wallet, and his driver's license. Frank, always hating birthdays, said his birthday was on February 29th, a Leap Year, but the date on the license was February 28th, not the 29th as he had claimed. On his sixty-fifth birthday, I gave him dinner at our favorite restaurant. I had the birthday cake made to resemble the Social Security card he'd never had since he never worked. That birthday celebration he loved and spoke of often. The difference in the dates I discovered was a perfect example of Frank Martin Tack. As enigmatic in death as in life.

I had never experienced a loss like that. I grieved both of my parents, Barry, and others, of course, but when Frank died his absence felt seismic. Emotionally devastated, I called his sister Lois at her home in Sewickley, Pennsylvania, to notify her of her brother's death. The following day, while waiting for the plane, I saw a woman walk out and realized she looked exactly as Frank would have looked in drag. I waved, and when she came over to me, she quickly apologized for having packed so hurriedly that she'd forgotten to bring gloves. I assured her that in California women no longer wore them. After making chit-chat in the car, I dropped her at her hotel as she wanted to rest rather than go out to dinner. The following morning, I picked her up and drove her to Frank's house. When we arrived, she took one look around and said, "Why did he need such a big house?"

Frank and Lois's mutual uncle Augustus Tack had been a turn-of-the-century landscape painter whose work was in the Phillips Gallery Collection in Washington, D.C. As I showed her around the place, I mentioned the painting, which she barely glanced at and then quickly put in her large handbag.

After Frank's body was cremated, she and I drove to pick up the ashes, and she immediately took them back to Pittsburgh to put in the family vault. There was no final meal or opportunity to sit with or hold his ashes, and I never heard from her again until Frank, who had donated a Ruffatti pipe organ to Mary Davies Hall, was to be honored by the San Francisco Symphony a year later, and I was asked to invite his sister and Frank's friends.

Despite still harboring some resentment toward her, I reserved a hotel for Lois and hired a limousine to take us to the concert hall. On the way there, sitting side by side in the back seat of the car, she turned to me with a sneer and said, "What in the world was Frank doing knowing a Jew like you?"

The limo driver's head jolted around, and I calmly said, "Thirty-six years, that's what."

We didn't speak to each other for the rest of the evening, but when I returned to my hotel room I sobbed.

I called Frank's lawyer the following morning to tell him what had happened, and he advised me not to contact her or answer any of her letters, saying he would take care of it. A few days later, I received a call from a woman introducing herself as Eleanor Smith. "Yes," she said, "my name is Smith, but I am Jewish too and trust me, we know how to handle a woman like that." It seems during her trip to California, Lois had asked Frank's houseman about me and was told I was Jewish. She hadn't known Frank was gay or didn't want to know, but she now knew I had been his partner and was also a Jew. It was then that I realized why he always had called her his "hated sister Lois."

Every relationship is different, and because Frank's and my relationship was open, many of our friends didn't know we were still together because they often saw or heard about us with other people. But Frank and I knew.

A close friend, John Wells Ireys, was gracious enough to loan me his beautiful house to give a memorial party in Frank's memory. Scotty Bowers, who had always been the bartender at Frank's and our friends' parties, poured drinks for thirty of us. At the end of the evening when I went to pay Scotty, he said he could never accept the money because he had adored Frank and was just happy to be of service.

Nobody ever said an unkind word about Frank, which is what made some of his behaviors toward me all the more mystifying and difficult to reconcile. We had thirty-six years of loving each other but never truly understood what we meant to one another.

Bobby Short had a house in Mougins, France, and soon after Frank died, he called me to express his sympathy. "You know, I have a house in Mougins with a wonderful piano," Bobby added. "Why don't you come by this summer and play for me?"

It was the perfect opportunity to take some much-needed time and space to process the loss of Frank. In France, I reflected on our tumultuous relationship, realizing he was the only person who knew everything about me and who had loved me. Even though we'd battled, he was the one person I could depend on in a crisis. Now, there was no one left to turn to. I had always tried to make him proud of me but still wondered if I'd succeeded. They say that part of grief is unresolved communication, and getting comfortable with unanswered questions, and I had to accept that there were certain things I might never know.

From then on, my relationship with Bobby grew from being a mere acquaintance to a real friend. Each time I was in New York I would drop by the Carlyle where he performed, sit at the bar, and wait until he was finished when we would sip our drinks and catch up on our lives. The following summer I took him up on his Mougins invitation beginning an annual three-day visit, but never longer, having gotten the hint after he told me about an American couple we knew who visited him every summer. "They're like the swallows of Capistrano arriving always on the same date." Upon arriving, I was always given a guest bedroom in the basement, and, one summer, I complained about the room being dark and dank. Bobby stared at me and said, "If it's good enough for Gloria (Vanderbilt), then it's good enough for you!" Touché. He must have appreciated my candor—or forgot my faux pas—because the following year I was given a bedroom on the main floor with lots of light.

When we drove to dinner, Bobby would often pop a cassette into his car's stereo system and play a new unreleased recording of his. It was thrilling to hear him sing along with his voice on the tape. Bobby never had learned to read music, having played by ear since he was a child. One summer, when I arrived at the house, he handed me a piece of sheet music and asked me to play it so he could hear the song. I played it exactly the way it was written. He pushed me off the piano bench, sat down, and played it in his unique Bobby Short style. My jaw dropped. To my amazement, he'd remembered the song note for note.

During those trips to Mougins, his houseguests were always included in the numerous invitations he received to dinners and parties. I attended many such events, including a dinner at Lynn and Oscar Wyatt's in Beaulieu, or at the Sacklers' in Antibes, among other glittering evenings. Once, at a luncheon in Antibes, there were just four of us present—the hostess, her husband, and the two of us. As dessert watermelon was served, Bobby whispered to me, "Do I dare?" He was irreverent about his skin color, often emphatically stating he was Negro and not black or African American.

In a patisserie in Cannes one morning, a French woman asked him, "Are you Bobby Short?"

"Yes," he said.

Delighted, she said, "Oh, my husband and I always go to the Carlyle to hear you."

At that, a tall man with a booming American voice standing behind her said to Bobby, "My wife thinks you are the best. . . . Glad to meet you. My name is Admiral Maure and that's my ship the *SS Eisenhower* out there in the bay."

Bobby introduced me to the Admiral, who invited us to come aboard the next day. On the way back to Mougins, I told Bobby it felt like one of those World War II movies and joked that I could go as Carole Lombard, and he could go as the polka dot bikini starlet Chili Williams (his Dalmatian dog was named Chili).

Early the next morning, we drove into Cannes where we were

warmly welcomed aboard by *GQ*-like sailors dressed in faded blue jersey shorts and tight white T-shirts. The good-looking crew and special uniform had been personally chosen by the Admiral's wife, whom everyone called Madame, to run the launch. Once aboard, we met the captain and were given a personal tour of the ship staffed with six thousand sailors, most of whom were a bunch of pimply-faced teens, a far cry from the sexy sailors who had greeted us.

It was a very special day. We were given a tour of the ship, including the galleys, and allowed to sit in a fighter plane. A few African American musicians on the ship recognized Bobby, and once word got out that he was there, some of the kids invited us to come back that evening because they were giving a concert onboard, but Bobby graciously declined their offer.

The following night at the Nice Jazz Festival, a few of the sailors from the ship came over to say "hi." Then Bobby and I went backstage where he was warmly greeted by the members of the Count Basie Orchestra and the vibraphonist Lionel Hampton, who told us to take our seats on the stage near the band arena. As I sat there, I looked out at the audience in the ancient open-air arena hoping there might be someone I knew who would see me, Larry Chrysler from the projects in Minneapolis, Minnesota, sitting with that illustrious orchestra on the stage in Nice, France.

It was always hard to leave France. The AIDS epidemic had spread worldwide, and whenever I returned to Los Angeles it seemed another close friend was on death's doorstep. Of course, Frank was still on my mind, grief deep in my heart. When someone close to you dies, particularly by suicide, you don't know how you are grieving. Suddenly everything in LA was getting to me, the traffic, the people, my life, my consulting job, everything. Now I know it was grief, but I didn't realize it at the time. In Mougins, I could escape it for just a little bit, even if it was only for a few days.

In Los Angeles, it seemed like every time I turned a corner I'd be reminded of Frank. There were still so many daily reminders that it was nearly impossible to "move on." Frank had named me his executor and I had to deal with his lawyers and bankers, again faking a role I wasn't sure how to play. His house was put up for sale and as I wandered through the rooms, I opened a bedroom closet and saw hanging in a neat row the suits and blazers I'd insisted he buy from my English bespoke tailor friend. All unworn. In a desk drawer was also a file with copies of the *Daily News Record*, the fashion industry newspaper that had interviewed me on numerous occasions. He'd kept them all, just like my mother had kept the clippings of me from the paper when I played the piano for Arthur Rubinstein and a shop owner as a kindergartner. I sat and cried knowing he had been interested in my professional life and success after all.

Around this same time, a close friend of mine, the decorator Kalef Alaton, discovered he had AIDS and was moving out of his Santa Barbara/Montecito weekend rental house. He called and suggested that since I'd always liked it there so much, I should consider selling my house and moving into his rental.

I thought it was a great idea, an offer to take me away to a very beautiful place where I could change my life, relax, and so forth, and I put my house on the market almost immediately. It turned out to be a very hot market, and my house sold the day it was listed for six times what I'd paid for it ten years earlier. You just can't plan luck like that. I was very fortunate.

When the movers left, I packed up my German Shepherd and drove to my new home situated on two acres in a bucolic canyon. My dog ran free, and for the first time since I could remember, I breathed freely.

TWENTY-FIVE

Past Life Therapy

At a party in Santa Barbara, I met a psychologist involved in an experimental study at UCLA regarding the effect of supposed past lives on our present, and whether past lives were an influence on our fears and emotions. After chatting for a while, he said that taking part in the study might help participants better understand themselves. I'd always been interested in alternative spiritual beliefs, like astrology, angels, and past life regressions, and I knew there had been many books written about past lives, but I had no idea they were studying it in universities and conducting actual clinical experiments.

I immediately signed up for three sessions, each of which was an incredible experience for me. At my first session, I went to the psychologist's office whom I'd met at the party. After a brief interview, he explained I was to lie down on a couch, relax, and that he would then attempt to hypnotize me and record answers to questions he would ask while I was under hypnosis. I guess I was a good candidate for hypnosis because I was "asleep" in no time, and that's when I remember hearing his voice and answering his questions as if in a dream or a movie.

He hypnotized me on three different dates, and each time I returned home from those appointments, I immediately wrote down everything I could remember about the session and all the details about what I had experienced in my past life.

Wisconsin 1900s

Question: "Where are you?"

Answer: I am sitting under a tree.

Q: "What are you wearing?"

A: A big shirt, loose pants, and no shoes. I'm barefoot.

Q: "Why are you there?"

A: Because my dad found me in the barn fooling around with my girlfriend and he hit me. I ran out and am afraid to go home. Then the next thing I know I am at the home of a warm and comforting friend of my mother. She tells me I can stay with her and her family.

At that point, the doctor woke me, and we discussed the session. I asked him if this could be a long-lost recollection of one of my mother's friends.

"That is one of the questions we also have," he replied. "Could we have certain memories in our subconscious?"

However, it was only the woman in the story that seemed familiar.

New York—Orchard Street 1800s

Question: "What are you doing?"

Answer: I am sitting on the steps in front of our house waiting for my father to come home from work. He works in a grocery store.

Q: "How old are you?"

A: I am eleven.

The next thing I saw was an image of living in San Francisco as an adult and wearing a three-piece houndstooth-pattern suit, working as an architect. I was standing on a pier at the Embarcadero with a colleague looking at a warehouse I had designed when suddenly it caught fire. In my mind, I knew I had used faulty materials. Shocked, my colleague slapped me on the back, and I fell into the water. Afraid of drowning, I grappled with the moss-covered supports of the pier until, finally, some men pulled me out.

The next image was me drunk and thinking I'd best get home because my wife would be angry. We live at 1079 Stockton Street. She opens the door and the bright light from the interior blinds me temporarily. After I came out of the hypnosis, I told the doctor about my fear of drowning and thought it might be because of a recurring incident with my father when I was a child, when he would take me into the lake and throw me into the air and pretended he was going to drop me.

Could this be the real reason for my fear?

Virginia 1700s

Question: "Who are you?"

Answer: I am a small woman wearing an off-the-shoulder dress in the dining room of our house. My husband comes in. He is wearing the costume of the day: Breeches and a tricorne hat. I berate him for being late and tell him to hurry and change clothes because we have guests arriving for dinner. The dining room table is set with China and cutlery and behind it is a cabinet with glass doors exhibiting wine glasses. Next, I am standing behind a crowd trying to see the soldiers marching in the parade in front of us. It is difficult for me to see because I am so small. The soldiers are flying flags and are in uniform. A young boy is playing the drum.

Then, I am awakened.

———— ∾ ————

After my first session, I went to the Bodhi Tree bookstore in West Hollywood, which specialized in spiritual, alternative, and New Age literature. There were numerous books about past life regression, and I bought a copy of each one they had. I still wonder if this was my subconscious enabling me to live these episodes. However, each session was related to a certain part of my current being.

Overall, my experience with the past life study helped me to reframe and re-contextualize my life in a whole new way. I now had clear explanations for and confirmation of things I'd never quite been able to put my finger on but which I knew to be major factors and driving influences in my life, including displaying shiny glassware and polished silver in an upright 1700s-style cabinet. I'm still so grateful that man was brought into my life when he was, as what I learned from those experiences continues to inform how I interpret and make meaning of my life today.

TWENTY-SIX

Out Of The Blue

While living in Montecito I hadn't given up my Beverly Hills telephone number and was called by my friend Rosemary, the director of the fashion design school Otis-Parsons, who asked me if I'd be interested in teaching a class in dress design. Parsons! That was the school I could have never afforded when I first went to New York, and now I was being asked to teach at a branch of it. I readily accepted, on the condition that I could only teach one day a week since I'd be driving down from Santa Barbara. Out of the blue, another opportunity came my way. My angels had returned.

On teaching days, I'd drive down Benedict Canyon when I got to LA, passing by my old house every week which reminded me of the life I still had there. After a year of making that once-a-week commute, I realized my life was in Los Angeles. Santa Barbara was beautiful but boring, and each weekend I invited friends from LA to stay just so I wouldn't be alone. On Friday evenings, I'd hear the crunch-crunch of car tires on the gravel in the driveway, and then on Sunday when they all left, my dog Baron and I would take an exhausted nap. Montecito was beautiful, too, but there was nothing for me to do there other than go to the gym, have lunch, and get the mail out of the canyon road mailbox. The symphony, opera, and my friends were all in Los Angeles, so I moved back down and bought a house directly across the street from the house I'd sold.

I continued teaching each week until a student mentioned the name of an Italian designer unfamiliar to me. That was the moment I knew I was no longer in tune with the ever-changing industry and resigned from my position. I no longer cared if skirts were long or short or who was in or out. It was time for me to retire and live new dreams.

Free At Last

Officially retired but still single and restless, I began traveling the world. I took off first for Asia, a place I found fascinating, and then enjoyed many wonderful, life-affirming trips to Burma, North Africa, South Africa, and elsewhere. For two consecutive years in Florence, Italy, I took a month's intensive Italian language course. Then, another year, I went to the south of France where I took another month's course in French. If I were in Paris during Men's Fashion Week, I would still roam the exhibition halls just to stay in touch, and I loved going to London, where I rented a flat on Eaton Square for a month.

On one of those London trips, strolling back to my hotel in Mayfair, I passed by the legendary Café Royale when suddenly the doors flew open. Three couples in evening clothes, the ladies in long dresses and the men in tuxedos came out of the cafe and began to seriously fight on the sidewalk. It was completely surreal, like a scene from a movie: they were all hitting one another, the ladies hitting the men with their handbags, the men wrestling each other to the ground until a taxi pulled up in front of the cafe. Without further ado, the fight came to a sudden halt as one of the women screamed in a high-pitched English voice, "PEETAH!," grabbed a man by his arm, and dragged him into the taxi. The others brushed themselves off and smoothed their clothes out, then returned to the cafe.

The magazine *Time Out London* published a notice that the Broadway star Barbara Cook would be appearing at a local seedy gay bar. Given the type of bar it was, I suspected it might be a female impersonator and not Barbara Cook herself, and I thought it would be fun to see. Two friends and I decided to go and, much to our surprise, it was indeed Barbara Cook and her accompanist, Wally. She sang to an enthusiastic, boozy audience and, after her set, I went up to her and explained I was a fan from Los Angeles, then invited her and Wally to the bar for a drink.

"What the hell are you doing in a place like this?" I asked her.

She smiled, then said, "My idiot agent booked me without knowing what kind of a club it was. He just said, 'Pack your bags, Barbara, you're going to London!'" She then roared with laughter and put us all at ease. "But what's not to love?" she said. "I'll sing for you guys any day of the week."

We had another drink before she took the stage again for another set, singing my favorite song upon request, "Wait Till You See Her."

Before my time in London came to an end, Bobby Short telephoned, asking me to stop in New York for a two-fold event weekend. He was throwing a cocktail party to celebrate his Mougins housekeeper who had worked for him for twenty-five years and was inviting all his former summertime guests whom she knew. It was also to be Bobby's birthday, and a friend of his was separately giving him a black-tie dinner dance in an Upper Eastside restaurant.

It was Madame Clement's first trip to New York and Bobby put her up at the Carlyle Hotel, complete with a car and driver as needed. When I arrived at the party, Madame Clement said to me, "*Oh Monsieur Chrysler, vous être le seul personne qui parle Français (You are the only person here who speaks French).*" She seemed a bit disoriented not being able to converse in English with the other guests, none of whom spoke French, and was relieved I was there.

The following day, I was invited to join Bobby and Madame Clement for lunch at the posh restaurant La Grenouille. We were seated in the VIP first room on a banquette and next to us was a well-tailored man looking like he might be the CEO of a major corporation. He greeted Bobby and Bobby said, "You do know Madame Clement?"

"*Ah bonjour, Madame, (Ah, good day, Madam)*" the man replied.

I laughed to myself thinking, yes, that was Bobby introducing his housekeeper and making everyone feel comfortable, celebrity or not. At one point during the lunch, Madame Clement turned to me and, looking across the room, excitedly said, "*Regarde! Il-y-a Henri Kiss-son-jay (Look! There is Henry Kissinger)!*" How she recognized Henry Kissinger, when she barely spoke English, I will never know.

While Madame Clement had been in New York she had been royally entertained, and the next time I stayed in the Mougins house she burned my ears with tales of her adventures there.

Bobby's gala birthday party was held at the iconic eatery Mortimer's, and they had closed the whole restaurant to the public for that evening. I was dressed in my Armani tux and looked spiffy entering with the elite of New York, whose attendees included many high-profile celebrities, including Lauren Bacall. When I asked her if she remembered me, she said, "Of course I do. You choked on a peanut when we were at the Flore in Paris."

The small orchestra was seated on top of the bar, playing throughout dinner and well into the wee hours as everyone danced the night away. The first person on the dance floor after dinner was Miss Bacall, who was being whirled around by Bobby's tall, heavyset brother, and screaming, "Help, help, help!"

What I loved about my friendship with Bobby was how easy and natural it was, how much fun we had, and that I could be myself with him regardless of whether we were at his home in Mougins or a party in New York City. When I was with Frank, I was always an "and" (This is Frank *and* his friend Larry; This is Frank, oh, *and* Larry.). But when I was with Bobby, I became ME, Larry Chrysler, and that was such an empowering feeling.

TWENTY-SEVEN

The Soviet Union

I'd read an article in *The Wall Street Journal* about Slava Zaitsev, a clothing designer for the elite in the Soviet Union, and decided to go to Moscow and interview him with the idea of selling it to *Menswear Daily* magazine.

To arrange the meeting in advance of my leaving for the USSR, I called a former model of mine who was now the personal secretary for Armand Hammer, an industrialist who'd been a close friend of Lenin, asking her to set up the interview. She called back saying she was told it was impossible. Not to be dissuaded, I telephoned the Soviet embassy in Washington, D.C., asking the same question, and got the same answer, "Impossible! He is too busy."

Luckily, American Express's London offices had a tour to the USSR that coincided with my travel dates to Europe, and they were able to include me with their tour group. However, I needed a visa to enter the country which would have taken more time to get than my schedule allowed, so I telephoned my friend at Hammer's office, and within the week I had my visa. With the visa in hand, I decided

I would try to get an appointment when I arrived in Moscow.

I stopped in New York on my way to London and ran into a French friend I'd known in the fashion business. When I told him where I was headed, he said his wife was involved in the Refusenik Movement (helping Jews unable to leave the Soviet Union) and asked if I'd be interested in being a courier, which entailed bringing medicine and clothing to the Soviet Union and in return being given secret information I would then pass on to a contact in Europe upon my return. It all seemed so frightening, but I felt I had to do it. I was Jewish, after all, and these were struggling Jewish people who were not allowed to leave the Soviet Union at that time. It was an opportunity to help them improve their lives in some small way. So, I said yes. He thanked me and said I would be contacted by someone in London and given further instructions.

Much to my relief, I never received a call.

Before leaving London for Moscow, we were given information regarding what to expect about life in the USSR. One of the most striking bits was that there would be no Russians in our hotel because they were forbidden to associate with foreigners. Before I left, I'd already been advised by a friend against any "personal" contact with the citizens. Information that proved useful.

The interior of the Aeroflot plane was a single large cabin with rows seating ten across. The crew, sitting in the front row for most of the trip, wore white nylon shirts and sky-blue skirts and trousers. Occasionally, a flight attendant would push a cart down the aisle asking if we would like a beverage, but otherwise, the crew made themselves scarce, so much so that I wondered who in the hell was flying the plane. We arrived safely at a dimly lit Moscow airport, and before we could leave the airport our baggage was opened and inspected by authorities. Once again, watching them go through my things, I was glad I'd never received that call to bring extra provisions in exchange for "secrets." We departed the airport in buses for a hotel with a thousand rooms, where on each floor was a fierce and strong-looking woman sitting at a desk in front of the elevator—for what purpose, I never found out. The room itself was sparsely furnished and, having been told before leaving London that the rooms were electronically bugged, each time I walked into the room I made a point of looking at the ceiling and loudly saying, "I love it here. I love it here."

The following morning, I went to the Intourist traveler desk in the hotel lobby stating I was from the *Los Angeles Times* (a white lie), and that I would like to make an appointment to interview the designer Zaitsev at the company Dom Modeli.

"It is not possible to have an appointment," the agent told me matter-of-factly. "However, should you like to go to see the displays of the clothes, that would be possible."

I said I would like to go and requested a translator to accompany me. The agent said they had French-speaking personnel at the design house who would translate, but I politely said I was more comfortable with an English-speaking person. I'd been previously told Intourist was infiltrated with the KGB and figured God only knew what might happen if I went there without an English-speaking translator.

I anxiously waited in the lobby at the appointed hour. Presently, the double doors opened and a petite blonde woman holding a large wet umbrella introduced herself and said, "It is raining cats and dogs." (I later learned this is the first English translation in the Russian language book.) After carefully explaining my request, we then took a taxi to the design house on Kuznetsky Most Street.

We arrived at a six-story, drab concrete block building with the sign: Dom Modeli. When we entered, we were stopped by a woman sitting at a desk asking why we were there. I explained with the help of the translator and was told, "Impossible!" She then pointed to a large room with showcases exhibiting female and male department store-type mannequins wearing a variety of clothing and was told we could go in there to see his work.

My translator apologized to me and said, "Better than nothing, yes?" And it was. Having seen many collections and having been a clothing designer, I figured I could remember what I was seeing and then do quick sketches as soon as I returned to my hotel room.

While I was wandering around the showcases, a tall heavyset man came up behind my translator and whispered something to her. She then turned to me and said, "This is Mr. Zaitsev and he would be happy to give you an interview." Shocked and caught off guard, I shook his hand. He said he was delighted to meet me. It turned out he was not impossible to interview after all. He led us to an employee cafeteria where we drank coffee and chatted. His English was perfect American English, and he regaled me with a story of how the French designer Thierry Mugler came each year, bringing him the latest music CDs and news of the West, in turn being shown all of Zaitsev's new creations. *Aha!* I thought. *I wonder if I have found Thierry's secret design source.* At the end of the interview, he gave me a small portfolio with his picture and bio, then invited me to the opening of his new collection that very evening. I suggested I bring my translator and he agreed. She said she'd have to miss her scheduled dinner but had no trouble canceling it since this was a once-in-a-lifetime experience for her having not been one of the elites.

When we arrived back at the Dom Modeli building at the appointed hour, Zaitsev was at the entrance and escorted us backstage to meet the tall, beautiful female and male models waiting to start the show. We were then seated at the end of the runway—a very special position normally reserved for VIPs. As I looked around the room, I saw stylishly attired men and bejeweled women dressed like no one I had seen among the very poor people walking the streets of Moscow. This was the elite of the USSR. The fashion show began, and I was pleasantly surprised to see how exciting and well-made the clothes were, easily competing with anything I'd seen in Paris.

Returning to the hotel at a late hour, I went into the first-floor bar and ordered a vodka (Stolichnaya being the "well" vodka) and a caviar sandwich. Sitting and eating on a long banquette I was soon joined on one side by a swarthy bearded man and on the other by a tall blond man.

"Where are you from?" asked the bearded man in a heavy Russian accent.

"California," I said.

Then, in a voice that became increasingly louder, he said numerous times, "I am Jew. I want to go to America," and then asked me if I knew anybody named Mizrahi in New York.

"No," I said warily, having been told Russian citizens were not allowed to be in hotels with foreigners. The blond then told me not to pay attention to him because he was drunk. Then, suddenly, another man arrived and stood in front of me shouting, "I am Palestinian! Do you go to Israel?"

At that, I realized I'd become a target for these men and shakily excused myself. I was so unnerved that I immediately went upstairs to the second-floor bar and downed a double vodka.

The next evening, I was with my travel companions in another of the numerous hotel bars. I wanted to sit but there were no chairs and only one sofa, which was partially occupied by a young man feverishly smoking a cigarette. I sat down next to him. Then, as if in a Peter Sellers movie, I turned my head to see a man look at me and then suddenly duck behind a nearby pillar. This happened a few times before my travel companions and I decided to leave for dinner.

A few days later in Paris, relieved to be out of the USSR, I related my story to my friend whose wife was involved in the Refusenik Movement and was very knowledgeable about the USSR. He told me that I'd been set up because I had not had official permission to obtain my interview and had been given forbidden printed material. The month before my arrival, an American journalist had been jailed for that very reason. In other words, my friend told me, I was beyond lucky to have gotten out of the country.

My angels had worked overtime to save me from another scrape.

TWENTY-EIGHT

Art And Murders

Several years before retirement, I began buying art, and my collection grew into something I took great joy in curating and adding to. It included bronze sculptures by the Italian Bruno Romeda; 'La Trinite', an Art Deco piece created by Jan and Joël Martel; a wonderful Rauschenberg; a Hockney I'd found at a small gallery in Paris; and Latin American sculptures and paintings, among them two large oeuvres by Cuban artist Bekis Ayón. A Los Angeles gallery owner, Tere Itturalde, arranged a trip to Mexico to visit galleries and museums in Mexico City and Monterey, and that trip was the beginning of a relationship of sorts that I could have never imagined.

On our first morning in Mexico, a group of twelve of us were waiting in the lobby of the Four Seasons Hotel ready to go on the tour, when Norman Blachford and his guest, who'd arrived on a different flight, joined the group late just as we were about to leave. Norman was a close friend of mine, but I had no idea who his guest was, and he hadn't mentioned anything to me about him. They casually walked down the hotel staircase, and when they reached the group, Norman presented us to his young friend, Andrew da Silva.

Andrew was very well-dressed in an expensive sports coat and, given my fashion eye, the most notable thing t noticed about him was his socks. I immediately knew they were from the Italian company Zegna because I owned a similar pair. I knew how much they cost, too, and I was impressed at what good taste the young man had. Throughout that day, Andrew regaled us with stories about his extensive travels, freely dropping well-known names. To my cynical mind, it sounded like fabrications given the fact that he was so young and there was no way he could have possibly experienced so much in his short time on earth. It seemed he felt compelled to impress us, and I felt obligated, as a good friend of Norman's, to let him know my feelings regarding Andrew's tales.

At an appropriate time, I told Norman that I valued our friendship and wanted him to be happy, but that I thought he needed to be careful with Andrew. Norman immediately took offense and said I was mistaken. Andrew was charming, had a wonderful sense of humor, and was a good companion. Well, I'd said what I needed to, and from that moment forward, I had to accept Norman's choice and simply try not to let it bother me too much. But it can be hard to stand back when people you care about make poor choices. Every chance he had, Andrew held court with outlandish claims about his "glamorous" life, none of which were remotely believable.

A few months later, Norman telephoned me saying he'd heard I had rented a house for June in Saint-Jean-Cap-Ferrat, France, and that it had three bedrooms. He asked if I would like to share it with him and Andrew for the entire month. Norman was a very close friend, and I'm loyal to my friends, so I took his offer seriously despite my misgivings about Andrew. I considered what a month with him would be like. In the end, I suppose my loyalty and curiosity got the best of me because I agreed to the rental terms.

That June, I picked up Norman and Andrew at the Hotel Negresco in Nice and we drove to Cap Ferrat to meet the rental agent. The house was situated down a narrow dirt road directly above the beach—the only house in that locale on the sea. The pool was on a lower level with a pool house and bar, separated from the beach by a wire fence. When we looked over the fence to the sea, we saw nude men lying on the sand and large rocks. This was the gay nude beach in Saint-Jean-Cap-Ferrat!

On our first evening together, we drove into Nice to have dinner on the terrace of the popular restaurant Le Safari. Andrew was seated on my left and Norman was facing him. Dinner was served, and as we drank our white wine, I turned to Andrew and said if we were going to spend a month together I wanted him to know that I felt there was no way at his relatively young age he could have done all of the things he said he did, nor could he have gone to all of the places in the world and known all of the famous people he had mentioned previously. Andrew did not say one word but held his wine glass and stared straight ahead at Norman. At the time, I thought how strange it was that he didn't reply, or even appear upset, showing no emotion whatsoever.

The month went by with friends visiting, exploring the Côte d'Azur, and Andrew being attacked by fleas in his bed, but otherwise, it was a good time for all. Each evening, when Norman and I retired to our bedrooms, Andrew would go down to the pool house, smoke a cigar, and read magazines. One day, there was a conversation about the Marrakesh Hotel Mamounia, where I had stayed a few times. I was describing the decor and beautiful gardens when Andrew blurted out, "Oh, I once loved the hotel but now nobody who is anybody goes there anymore. It just isn't done."

As he spoke, I realized he was quoting an interview with Yves Saint Laurent's partner Pierre Bergé in an English fashion magazine I had left on the dining table the day before. His comment was another one of his supposed experiences—and an obvious lie. I felt certain he'd never been there. Another of his fantasies was when it was his turn to shop for groceries, and I complained that the price he'd paid for certain items was outrageous, he blithely claimed he never looked at the price of anything because in his "very rich" family there was no need.

One evening, the three of us, along with our two houseguests, drove into nearby Nice to go to L'Ascenceur, a gay bar I frequented when in town. The moment we entered the bar, Andrew, in a booming voice, said, "Well, here we are fellas, the rich American guys from California." It was mortifying.

Happily, the rest of the month was uneventful, and Andrew continued his nightly time alone reading and smoking in the pool house.

Norman and I belonged to a private international gay businessmen's club called Gamma Mu. Twice each year the members gathered in a US city hosted by resident members where we spent four days going on special tours, participating in meetings, and networking and socializing with each other. At the requisite Friday luncheon, new members were introduced. Before the seated group, each person explained where he was from, who had sponsored his membership, and what their type of career was. This particular Fly-In (as they were called) was in Seattle, and Norman brought Andrew, who had recently become a new member. That Friday, the newbies stood before the crowd and rattled off the usual list: their sponsor, their hometown, and their career. Except for Andrew.

When he stood on the stage, he said, "My name is Andrew da Silva. I am from La Jolla, California, and I don't work. Norman Blachford, my sponsor, keeps me."

A collective gasp filled the room. The next morning, I saw Norman with his luggage in the lobby, where he was checking out of the hotel. He said he and Andrew were leaving early because there was an emergency and they had to return to California. I knew, however, that Norman was embarrassed and couldn't stand the thought of saving face for the rest of the weekend.

I rarely saw Andrew after that except for a dinner or two with Norman here in Los Angeles. Then, the shocking news came on the television about Andrew, whose real last name was Cunanan: he had been murdering men in Minneapolis and his whereabouts were unknown.

An FBI agent stationed in Minneapolis called me and informed me my name was found on a list of Andrew's intended victims. He said to contact the authorities immediately if anything came up and promised to reach out to me should it be found that I was in any danger. After that call ended, I put the telephone down and began to shake all over.

Meanwhile, there were television interviews with purported "friends" of Andrew's relishing their fifteen minutes of fame, telling untrue stories about him and their friendships just as Andrew had spread his false stories over the years. Each time I called Norman, he would repeatedly say, "Oh it couldn't possibly be our Andrew." His denial was the same as it had been when I had originally warned him about Andrew in Mexico City.

In New York on my way to Europe shortly after the news first broke, things continued to remain tense and frightening with Andrew still on the loose, his whereabouts still unknown, and a lot of murmurs "on the street" that he might be in New York City. My greatest fear was he might be out to get me because of that evening at the restaurant in Nice when I called him out on his lies.

Norman phoned and said he would be in New York at the same time as me. When I asked him where he was staying, he named the same hotel he and Andrew usually stayed in, which was on a dark and quiet street near the Plaza Hotel. Incredulous, I asked, "Are you out of your mind staying there? You could be accosted by Andrew on that street. He knows exactly where you stay."

Again, Norman poo-pooed the danger he might be in and then invited me to a cocktail party he was throwing at the Regents bar (A branch of the Tokyo bar with the same name). Bewildered by his continued denial, I put on my blazer and hailed a taxi to the bar.

About fifteen of us stood around the bar waiting for the oft-late Norman and all chatting about Andrew. We waited and waited until finally, about forty-five minutes later, Norman arrived with a new boyfriend, in tow: Peter. We all immediately eyeballed each other knowingly, because Peter's coloring and demeanor resembled Andrew's to a T.

Shortly after that, Gianni Versace was murdered in Miami, and the suspected killer was Andrew. I received a telephone call in LA from a person identifying himself as a friend of a friend. He felt he should tell me he had recently been at a dinner party in Rome given by the mayor of that city and that the conversation was about Versace's murder. The consensus was it was not Andrew who was the murderer but the Italian Mafia because Versace and his sister Donatella wanted to end their involvement with the company due to frequent allegations it was being financed as a money laundering entity and open a small company on their own. The name of the new company would be Sunshine.

This made perfect sense because it had been speculated among those in the American fashion industry as well that the Mafia might have financed the Versace operation. Given the low volume of merchandise rumored to have been sold in Versace stores, it couldn't possibly have supported the numerous retail outlets around the world. The stores were outrageously expensive to build and maintain. One in Berlin was owned by a friend of mine, who had given me a tour of the store and explained the extensive custom work that had been done and the artisans involved.

Meanwhile, the television news reported that the police continued to hunt for Andrew. A tip eventually led the authorities to storm a luxury houseboat docked in Miami Beach, where they found Andrew dead of a self-inflicted gunshot wound. His face had been shattered by the bullet, rendering him unidentifiable except for fingerprints. I never understood why, if he did kill Versace, what his motive was. He didn't even know him, and, contrary to the news reports, had never even met him. Knowing Andrew as well as I did, there is not a doubt in my mind that he would have bragged in detail about knowing Versace had they ever met.

About a year after Andrew's death, I was sitting at the counter in a coffee shop here in Los Angeles and happened to glance over at a person wearing a baseball cap eating lunch. I did a double-take, thinking he looked exactly like Andrew. He looked up and saw me staring, and I looked away wondering if I should call the police or if I should walk over to him and casually tell him I liked his cap. I thought if I did, and it was truly Andrew, I would have fainted dead away. So, I walked out, doing nothing. Had he been alive, I'm certain Andrew would have had the chutzpah to move to Los Angeles and move freely about. I still don't believe he killed Versace, but all the other murders, certainly.

TWENTY-NINE

A Paris Life

Paris was still a magnet, and I found myself going there more and more often, sometimes staying as long as three months in a rented apartment. I liked the idea of using the city as a base to visit other European countries and eventually decided to look for an apartment to buy. My dream was to own a small and simple pied-à-terre in Saint-Germain-des-Prés.

Unlike the United States, where we have a Multiple Listing System available to all real estate agencies, France has no centralized database. There are numerous agencies on almost every block with pictures of apartments and prices shown in the windows, and an apartment for sale in the same building as the agency might be unknown to the agents in the office below. Also, if you asked the agent to show you apartments, they would show a few in your category without ever calling back or maintaining a relationship with the potential buyer.

The concept of staging was entirely foreign. The flats often had unmade beds, underwear on the floor, dirty dishes in the kitchen, and a blaring television (also on the floor). Almost every agent's attitude was one of utter ennui; they couldn't be bothered. At the beginning of my search, I was introduced to an ex-editor of *French Vogue* (the widow of a nobleman) who, with a group of like-minded ladies, was finding apartments for foreign buyers. During two days of looking at apartments, none of which were within my budget, she told me about her stepchildren who hated her and the entire history of her deceased husband's renowned and hyphenated name.

Every morning, I scoured the advertisements for apartments in the newspaper *Le Figaro* and looked at ads in a free newspaper in the bookstore WH Smith on the Rue Rivoli. Without any success, I returned to Los Angeles and continued looking on Thursdays, perusing the sale ads in *Le Figaro* sold at a Sunset Blvd newsstand. The following year, I returned to Paris and browsed agency windows, returning each day to one on the rue de Rennes. I'd ask if there was anything in my budget, only to be told there was nothing available in the area until someone died—and even then, it was likely to be left to an heir.

As I walked the streets, I frequently looked up at the apartment building windows hoping to find something, but there would rarely be a *VENDRE* (For Sale) sign. If there was one, I would call the number and inevitably get the person's voicemail, where I'd leave a message which, of course, never got returned.

I began to lose hope, thinking I'd never fulfill my dream of owning property in Paris. The Hôtel de l'Abbaye in St. Germain was where I stayed when not renting an apartment; one morning, as I was reading the newspaper, I saw an ad for an apartment with an open house between noon and 1 p.m. that day. An open house was unusual for Paris, let alone for only one hour. The apartment for sale was located at 1 rue Cassette, just a few doors away from the hotel, which was at 10 rue Cassette.

As I passed through the lobby, I asked the manager, Madame Briki, if she'd like to view the apartment with me. Delighted, she accompanied me down the street. Directly on the street, a discreet dark green door opened to a small entry, and then to another door opening to a stairwell and a very small antique elevator. The apartment was the only one on the third (French) floor of the seven-story building. No one greeted us, so we proceeded to look around, seeing faded silk-covered walls, soiled carpets, exposed water tanks, and old electrical wiring, among many other outdated things. It needed a complete renovation. What the apartment did have was a perfect layout, which is a rare find in Paris. Often, large apartments are broken up. The toilet will be next to the kitchen—or even in a public stairwell. This apartment had a proper bath and a separate WC, a small living room, a larger dining room, a good-sized bedroom with built-in closets (another unusual feature for Paris), and a kitchen with a view overlooking the Mansard rooftops of nearby buildings. I immediately envisioned breaking down the wall between the living room and dining room, stripping all the mildewed ceiling moldings, and creating a modern place. The 1928 building was one of the first in Paris to be built of brick by the sculptor Jean Arp. The fact that Arp was a favorite artist of mine sealed the deal. It was kismet.

Madame Briki and I discussed the asking price, and she advised me on a reasonable offer. She then telephoned the agent and informed him that the apartment was a mess and needed an expensive renovation to even be habitable. Shortly after, he called back and said the owners had refused our offer. Undeterred, I continued my search. Then, a month later, the agent from the rue Cassette apartment called and asked if I was still interested in it. I said yes, but only at the price I had previously offered. He said he would have to work on the owner "psychologically" and would get back to me. The next day, he called and said they'd accepted my offer.

I was thrilled! But though I had read books about the complexities and headaches of buying property in France, nothing could have prepared me for what lay ahead in terms of navigating the bureaucracy and paperwork. *Mon Dieu*! And so, the adventure began.

Luckily, I had a friend who owned apartments in Paris and gave me sound advice, as well as the name of a reputable notaire. A notaire is a lawyer specializing in real estate or anything that requires legal government-signed papers. Their offices instigate a historical search of the property to be certain that it isn't beholden to any other ownership or laws, which, in my case, meant that they were looking to confirm that the nearby church of Saint Sulpice didn't still own the property as it had in God knows what year. In France, there is a ninety-day escrow period where within the first ten days of the offer the buyer has the right to cancel the purchase of the property. Also, should the buyer's bank refuse a loan on the property, the buyer may cancel. French law also states there must be a translator for foreign buyers to be sure all is understood in the reading of contracts. Finally, after much ado, a meeting was arranged at the office of the notaire for the signing of the papers, and I had my signed check for the required deposit of ten percent.

I intended to purchase the apartment with cash, but I'd been advised to say I was going to take out a mortgage, knowing this would allow me to cancel the deal within ten days by stating my bank would not subsidize the purchase. Otherwise, without this information, I could not cancel.

Seated at a round table with the notaire were me, the translator, and two agents representing the seller and his wife, who eyed me suspiciously throughout the meeting. My translator was a young lawyer whose English was barely proficient. However, one of the seller's agents spoke perfect English and smiled at me each time my translator attempted to translate. The owner was an older gentleman in a dark gray suit buttoned to the neck; he looked uncomfortable. His wife, who was about the same age, wore a silk print Saint Laurent dress with pearls and a perpetual grimace on her mouth.

After much discussion and reading pages of documents, the big question was posed: How was I to pay for the apartment? I replied with a bank mortgage just as I'd been instructed to do.

One of the agents sputtered "But but but, we were to understand you were to pay with cash."

"Oh no," I replied. "I must take a loan from my bank in Los Angeles. I still need to obtain a loan for the balance of payment."

There was a lot of huffing and puffing and speaking to one another and the notaire in very rapid French, none of which I understood. Haughtily, the owners relented and said since they had spent so much time with me, they would agree to the terms I wished. The promesse-de-vente was signed, and we shook hands. *Et voilà*! I was the proud new owner of a Parisian apartment.

As the owners and I walked out of the office, the wife turned to me and said, "*Monsieur, vous avez etes tres mechant avec le prix.*" (You have been very mean about the price.) I smiled and answered in French that the apartment needed a big renovation. With a huff, she answered, "*Bien! Chacun a son propre gout!*" (Well! Each has his own taste.) I nodded, smiled, and walked away clutching the keys to "my" new apartment.

Before the escrow closed, the agent allowed me to bring a young architect to plan the renovation. He was a charming French guy from the Riviera town of Hyeres and was just beginning to work in

Paris. His English was good, and I could communicate my ideas by fax from Los Angeles. Frequently, I would return to Paris to approve the work and further our discussions while going to stores to continue looking for furniture and appliances.

One of the biggest wholesale furniture and accessory exhibitions is Maison & Objet, which is held annually in an exhibition hall outside of Paris. Carrying business cards I'd had printed with my name, *Decorateur (Decorator)*, and my Beverly Hills address, I roamed the stands and aisles of the exhibition planning what to buy. One stand had beautiful, simple modern furniture. The name of the designer/owner was Catherine Memmi. Familiar with her store on rue St. Sulpice, I had often looked in the windows of her shop, both admiring and excited by her designs. So, I bit the bullet, walked on the stand, and was approached by an attractive blonde lady who asked if she might be of help.

"I am a decorator from Beverly Hills and am decorating an apartment on the rue Cassette in Saint Germain," I said. "Catherine Memmi has always been a favorite designer of mine."

She looked me in the eye and said, "Sir, I am Catherine Memmi." Then she extended her hand. "It's a pleasure to meet you."

At that, I gulped and immediately ordered a sofa, console table, and cocktail table. I guess you could say I was starstruck.

The workmen whom the architect hired would often work from 8 a.m. until 7 or 8 p.m. One evening, observing the demolition, I mentioned my surprise at their long hours. The foreman nodded and said, "We are Romanians. We are *not* French. They often leave early if they even show up at all." The apartment was finished in due time.

One of my dreams had always been to study piano in Paris with a French teacher who could show me how French music should be played. I now had an apartment large enough for a baby grand piano and began searching local piano stores hoping to find the perfect used piano. Finally, in the twentieth arrondissement at Le Centre Chopin, a store filled with used pianos, I found and settled on a black lacquer Yamaha.

Not considering how the movers would deliver the piano, I was assured by the salesman that this was Paris, and it was not unusual to deliver a piano to a third-floor apartment. A meeting was arranged for someone to come to the apartment to see the space.

"Oh, Monsieur, the elevator is too small," he said upon arrival. "We will have to bring it in through the window. Ça vas?"

I must have nodded, but it sounded so ridiculous to me. A piano? Through a window? In Paris?

"We will deliver at six o'clock before the morning traffic starts."

I then wrote in French on a large sign that there would be a slight amount of noise at such and such date and time and posted the notice on the mailboxes at the entrance. I was slightly worried I wouldn't be making the best first impression with my new neighbors, but, as the French say, "C'est la vie!"

At six in the morning on the designated delivery day, a worker called to say there was a flatbed truck on the street below my window, and because the window was so small, they would have to remove the "bar" below me. A bar is one of those fancy wrought iron balconies below numerous Paris apartment windows. However, the worker said, there was no need to worry—it would only take a short amount of time.

For the next two hours, the rat-tat-tat of an air gun trying to get the damned bar out of the brick building wall filled the entire building and streets around us. I was horrified, hoping that my neighbors, disturbed at that early hour, wouldn't be angry with me. At last, two men came running into the apartment, threw a medieval-looking pulley into the window with ropes hanging down, and then hoisted my piano into midair swinging above the morning rush hour traffic.

I had wanted to watch the procedure, but the scene was so nerve-wracking I went into my bedroom and closed the door, praying they knew what they were doing.

When I heard the piano being lowered onto the living room floor with the legs reattached, I breathed a sigh of relief. As soon as I thanked the workers and saw them out, I sat down at the piano and pressed a key.

Clink.

Then another.

Clunk.

It sounded horrible. Sickly. Broken.

I immediately called the Le Centre Chopin only to be told the piano had to "settle" a while after being delivered. In my best French, I let the guy have it.

"What, is the piano just going to tune itself while I'm sleeping?"

After relentlessly complaining, they finally agreed to send a technician out to tune my piano. *Tout suite*!

Now that I was ready to study French music in France, I was introduced to a teacher, Ivan, who was half-Brazilian and half-Swedish but who had lived in France for many years and was well-versed in the interpretation of French music. I was officially ready to begin my life as a Parisian, living part-time in Paris and part-time in Los Angeles. A dream come true!

THIRTY

Welcome To My Paris

One of the advantages of having an apartment in a place like Paris is the ability to deeply explore the city, develop friends who are locals, and entertain visitors from America and elsewhere. My apartment was a one-bedroom and unfortunately not well-suited for hosting guests. My sister, Sandy, for example, stayed in a nearby hotel whenever she visited.

Every September on his way back to New York after closing his Mougins house for the summer, Bobby Short would stay at the Hotel Ritz and we'd shop, dine, tour, and drink.

On one of our forays into the depths of the *Marche aux Puces* (flea market), I found two eight-foot-tall Chinese bamboo placards in black lacquer embossed with gold lettering that read when translated: *Enter with Peace*. Bobby said, "Buy them. They'll make the room!" When my petite, seemingly innocent young Filipina cleaning woman saw them hanging in the living room, she asked what the Chinese words said. I explained what I had been told by the antique dealer, to which she replied, "How do you know, sir?

They could say fuck you!" After I closed my dropped mouth, I laughed and realized she might have been right.

Before lunch one day, Bobby and I met at Café de Flore on the Left Bank for an apéritif. All of the terrace tables were occupied, so we went into the cafe where, sitting all alone directly in front of the entrance, was the actress Lauren Bacall. She warmly greeted Bobby and upon introducing me to her, he said, "You know Betty, don't you?"

Before I could even respond, she said, "Just sit down and have a drink!"

I'd heard that when Lauren Bacall became an actress, she had changed her name from Betty Joan Perske. However, her intimate friends still referred to her as "Betty." As the two old pals chatted, I had little to interject into the conversation, so when she took out a cigarette I asked if I might have one. I explained that I had quit smoking but that the only time I did was in Paris. She leaned into me with the unlit cigarette in her hand and her famously deep, signature voice said, "Me, too. It's like a movie, isn't it?"

Another time Jimmy Galanos was in town for a couple of weeks at the Hotel Plaza Athénée and called to ask if I would join him for dinner. Upon arriving at the reception desk, I asked them to telephone Mr. Galanos and inform him I was there. Well, I waited and waited. Again, the hotel clerk called Jimmy's room without an answer. Suddenly, an apologetic and distraught Jimmy rushed into the lobby saying he'd been locked in his bathroom, the phone could only be used to receive calls and not call out, so he opened the small bathroom window and began shouting for help both in French and English to no avail. Seeing his pants hanging on the door, he realized his wallet with credit cards was in the pocket. Remembering a movie he'd seen where the thief opened a door using a similar card, he reached into the wallet, took out the card, and opened the door. I gave him a reassuring hug, and we sauntered into the bar for a well-deserved before-dinner cocktail. He told me how much he liked the bar's ambiance and how, before bed each night, he went in for a Cognac or two (or three). I asked the price of a Cognac there and he airily replied, "Oh, about forty Euros I guess." I gasped, but I shouldn't have been surprised; after all, Jimmy Galanos only bought the best, and this was Paris's best.

During dinner, Jimmy mentioned he'd not been to the famous flea market in many years and would love to browse. I suggested we go the following day, and we agreed to meet in front of Café de Flore. Waiting at the designated spot the next morning, I saw a taxi arrive with Jimmy, who emerged from the backseat wearing sweatpants, a sweatshirt, a cap, and sneakers all in a matching shade of taupe. Very elegant and flea-market-ready. We still had to take the Metro to the market itself, and while we were standing in the crowded train, I noticed Jimmy looked uncomfortable but thought nothing more of it. We then spent several tiring hours wandering the aisles looking at antiques and bric-a-brac. As we were about to leave, he stood with his hands thrust into his pockets and adamantly announced he could *not* go through the Metro experience again so it would be best to take a taxi back to the hotel. I've always preferred to blend in wherever I was. I very much enjoyed being in Paris not as a tourist but living as a local, which meant things like taking the Metro or the bus when the situation called for it. The very stylish and elegant Jimmy Galanos, however, no matter how hard he tried to blend in, simply could not.

The Show Goes On

Seated across the desk from a travel agent in the Marais, I watched the agent speak to someone in very rapid French. Over and over, I heard the word "bomb." Distraught when she hung up the phone, she practically shouted at me explaining the New York World Trade Center had been attacked. On the way home, I noticed the street corner trash can's green liner already had been removed, a precaution against explosives. As soon as I walked into the apartment, an American friend, Bill Shaw, called asking if we should cancel our planned dinner for that evening.

"We have to eat," I said, "and I think it would be comforting for the four of us to be together, considering the circumstances in the United States."

When my friends arrived that night, the first thing I told them as I opened the door was, "Tonight we only speak French, we don't know if it is safe to be American here."

"But I don't speak French," Bill said.

"No problem," I said, "because we're going to an Italian restaurant anyway."

Under duress, my humor kicked in just as it always had in times of turmoil and crisis. We had no idea how to behave being so far from home.

In the following days, in shops and restaurants, upon hearing my American accent, strangers would tell me how sorry they were about the chaos in New York.

The American Club of Paris, founded by Benjamin Franklin and of which I was privileged to be a member, gave a lovely flower-strewn memorial on the Place d'Iena. A representative of the French government spoke of the enduring friendship between France and the United States. As I listened to him speak, my thoughts drifted to how proud I was to be an American, and yet how fortunate I was to be residing in France. It was both a terrifying and fascinating time to be living abroad. On the one hand, it strengthened my allegiance to my own country, and on the other hand, it opened my eyes to how the world truly saw America and Americans. For the most part, they wanted to see us overcome and recover, but there would always be that bit of a European grudge underneath the surface, those who don't align themselves with America but instead see it as an over-dominating force in the world. In the end, however, the mood in the air in Paris those years after 9/11 was one of fastidiously protecting their country and allies, and of peace and love towards all humanity.

In 2003, Bobby Short was turning 80 years old, so seven of us planned a "surprise" black-tie cocktail and dinner dance for eighty of his "closest" friends at the Rainbow Room high atop Rockefeller Center. However, the ever-clever Bobby found out about it and not only rearranged the assigned seating chart we'd put together but added a few more people to the list.

More than one hundred people mingled during the cocktail hour until dinner was called, at which point I escorted the opera singer Jesse Norman into the dining room. I'd met her before, and as we made our way to our assigned tables I cheekily mentioned how difficult it was to get tickets to her performances at the Chatelet Theater in Paris. She smiled and grandly replied, "Call me."

Among those seated at my table of eight was Gerry Stutz, the woman whose image Barry Bordofsky and I had emulated at the wild costume party back in the 1970s. She had been a retail idol of mine and now here she was, seated next to me.

As I looked around the large room, I thought of how it was not only the fiftieth anniversary of my first meeting Bobby, but also how I was now able to repay him for his many years of largesse, and how I, who had come so far in my life, was now comfortably seated among these glamorous people. A feeling of gratitude and contentment enveloped me for the rest of the very special evening.

At the end of the evening, without accompaniment, Jesse Norman stood and sang "Happy Birthday" to the birthday boy. It was nothing short of thrilling.

THIRTY-ONE

Looking For Love

When my sister Sandy died in 2004 of pancreatic cancer at a relatively young age, I began to contemplate my mortality, but before I could even think of moving on, I had to mourn my unpredictable sister.

I think of my life with Sandy, who was four years younger than me, as a series of episodes. Sandy and I had much in common. I am a gay man and she was a "lipstick" lesbian, and because of that dynamic, we had many mutual friends. She had been a sportswear designer while I was designing chic cocktail dresses. However, even with these and other similarities, our basic personalities were quite different. She was a much freer spirit than I ever could be, and this trait was often frustrating to me. I once admonished her for often forgetting where she put her house or car keys. Her answer to that was, "Yes, but think how often I don't forget them." Her habitual lateness in arriving at a designated time drove me mad. But with our many arguments, we knew we loved one another and always kissed and made up.

My mother often tried to foist her off on me to either take her to school when she was in grade school or during our early teens to school dances. As a child, Sandy was tiny; during the winter she would be bundled up in a snowsuit, resembling an overstuffed pillow. Angry at having to take her to school, I would drag her through the snowdrifts while she screamed, "Warry Warry." A little older we would make up "arias" in a pretend language; one I remember to this day was named *A Rima Cacheca L'Operaci.*

In 1951, the evening I returned from my first trip to New York, she asked me to tell her about the New York life I'd led and read to her what I had written in a diary I always carried. Little did I realize as I read from one page, another would flip up, enabling her to read the parts I'd skipped. When I closed the diary, she simply said, "You loved Frank Hill, didn't you?" I stammered and she assured me she still loved me because I was her brother, and she would always be there for me no matter who I was. A year or two later, I realized why she loved reading those *Wonder Woman* comics. It was then she fell in love with another girl.

Bi-sexual, Sandy would eventually marry a man and give birth to two lovely daughters, Danielle and Lisa. To this day, I tell my nieces stories of their mother—the fabulous and capricious Sandy Chrysler.

Yet at the time, I was often embarrassed by her individuality. When the other girls in junior high were wearing classic tan-colored camel hair coats, Sandy opted for a swirling gray wide-collared dramatic one. Classic, she was not.

Her lateness was exemplified while I was staying at the Plaza with Jimmy Galanos and she was over an hour late to join us for cocktails in the Oak Room bar. Finally, she and her girlfriend arrived heavily made-up and looking like hookers, both stoned on marijuana.

I suggested they order a drink and put it on my bill. Jimmy and I left the two of them sitting there.

After I moved out of Frank Tack's house, I threw a party in my apartment on Melrose Avenue. Sandy and two of her friends had been invited but they never showed up. On returning from dinner in a restaurant after the party, I noticed a new mattress that I'd bought and left leaning against a hallway wall was missing. A neighbor told me he'd seen Sandy and her friends take the mattress and tie it to the top of her car. Irate, I called her and said if she didn't return the mattress by morning, I was going to call the police. The mattress was promptly returned.

Our life together was eventful, to say the least, and in the end when she finally succumbed to the Pancreatitis disease the void left was insurmountable. I still miss arguing and laughing with her.

After she died, I realized that I was tired of having to call friends to travel with, go to dinners, and fill the sometimes lonely days and evenings. I'd come a long, long way from a poor kid to where I was now, and wanted to share the rest of my life with someone special.

When I told my Paris friends that I wanted to settle down with someone, they all said, "Oh, not you, Larry. The way you travel, and the way you live . . . " But I knew deep down that it was time, so, after a bit of research, I switched on my computer and signed up for a gay dating website.

I filled out a profile on the site, stating I lived in Paris and Los Angeles, but I didn't include my photo, because a trusted friend had told me it would help to filter out a lot of unwanted, sex-only, prospects. To my surprise, within days I received responses from all over Europe and the United States from some marvelous men.

But only one caught my attention AND he lived in Los Angeles. He said he'd been to Paris the month before and had fallen in love with the city, and he wondered what it was like living in both America and France. For three months, we wrote emails so extensive they practically became The Great American Novel. Once we were both comfortable enough, we exchanged photos and telephone numbers. When I saw his face for the first time, I was convinced he was the one for me. Even though we were presently over five thousand miles apart, he lived only fifteen minutes from my Benedict Canyon house. His name was Matthew Michael.

After I arrived back in LA and the jet-lag bags under my eyes had subsided, we arranged to meet in person for the first time at O Bar, a quiet bar and restaurant where I knew we could talk without having to shout over loud music.

I was both excited and slightly nervous the night of our first date. I knew we had a connection because we'd written so often in the previous months that I felt like we both knew each other inside and out. Yet meeting someone in person can be different than meeting them online, and I just hoped that we would feel as comfortable in each other's presence as we had via email and telephone.

That night, I walked into the bar and found him already waiting; to this day I still recall the cream-colored sweater he was wearing. Behind the barman was a large aquarium, and as we chatted, I mentioned how beautiful the fish were swimming in the lighted water. Matthew then began to tell me the names of each of the numerous types of fish, and I was very impressed. The only fish I could identify were the goldfish.

Because I've always been interested in astrological birth signs, I asked Matthew when his birthday was.

"February 28th," he said, and I practically fell off the barstool. It was the exact date of my late partner Frank's birthday, too. I thought,

Now I know all about you. I just hoped he didn't have the negative aspects of Frank's personality, like his obsession with privacy.

We continued our evening dining at a small table in the restaurant, and when it was time to leave, I thought, *Oh shit. I don't want him to see my $130,000 Mercedes AMG C32 in the parking lot and judge me by my car as so many people do in Los Angeles.* The fact was, I wasn't that rich; I'd leased the car on a whim. But he never even noticed it, and when we hugged goodbye, I watched him climb into a decked-out black Jeep. "Wow," I thought, "now that is hot!"

I'd done the precise thing I'd hoped he wouldn't do to me: judged him (ever-so-slightly) by his car. Fortunately, the conversation and attraction at dinner had been so great that his sexy car was simply icing on the cake.

Matthew and I began dating, and we had a wonderful time getting to know each other in person over the next few months. One day, as I was walking down the hallway in my house thinking about him, it suddenly occurred to me that I'd met him on the heels of my sister Sandy's death. I still remember exactly where I was in the hallway when I stopped in my tracks, looked up at the ceiling, and said, "Sandy, you sent him to me." Now she had joined my team of angels.

I eventually told Bobby Short that I was seeing someone and I thought it was becoming serious. Bobby didn't ask who, what, or where but, knowing me well, simply asked, "How old is he?" True, there had been a few younger boyfriends in my life, but I had never once thought of Matthew's age being twenty-nine. He was much more grounded than other younger men I had dated. He had a very good job and a degree in oceanography, he was sincere, and he adored his family. All of that and more were just a complete, undeniable package to me, and it gave me the desire to share an exciting part of my life with him.

Matthew moved into my Benedict Canyon house about six months later, and we became an official couple. When he met my family and friends, they immediately accepted him as my partner and adored him. Then it was time for his Catholic Republican family to meet me, a much older man and a Jewish Democrat. I joked that he should get ready to receive his inheritance early because they'd all have heart attacks and die when they met me. Luckily for all of us, there was no stress before the meeting. Matthew and I flew to Cleveland and met his folks at a casual restaurant. When I walked in, his parents smiled and said they were so happy to finally meet me, immediately dissolving any tension in the air. His father practically lifted me off the floor when he hugged me, and his brother, Bill, said I was not at all what they had expected. He called me a force of nature. A few years later, when Matthew and I married in 2013, we legally became a part of one another's families.

I had waited to meet the right person since Frank died in 1988, and, at long last, I did. I'm a big believer that, when it comes to love, patience wins the race. The fortunes that have blessed me during my life still astound me.

THIRTY-TWO

Letting Go

After I met Matthew, it became increasingly clear that keeping my apartment in Paris was no longer a prudent option. It became harder to go to Europe alone for stretches at a time while growing and maintaining my relationship with him, and I was being pulled in two directions. By this time, I wasn't walking well, and Paris is nothing if not a walking city. So, I began spending less and less time in Paris. We visited when Matthew had a summer break from his teaching job but the rest of the year, I found visiting Europe without him had become less pleasurable. Six years into our relationship, I bit the bullet and decided to sell the Paris apartment.

I thought I was savvy about the strict rules and regulations in France, but I was woefully unprepared for what they entailed. Selling an apartment in Paris was one of the many experiences abroad that was nearly incomprehensible to my American way of thinking. In my mind, the French seemed to thrive on bureaucracy. I was happy after the sale had gone through because I recalled each time that I arrived in Paris there had been a problem with one thing or another, and resolving those issues could take weeks or months, sometimes years. The Syndic (management), the water, the television, a leak, the electricity company—you name it. Living in France is not the same as being a tourist staying in a hotel or renting an apartment for a vacation, where one is not involved in the daily task of living in a foreign city. Some rules simply don't make sense.

In the end, I managed to jump through all the hoops and get out relatively unscathed by the French bureaucracy. I had lived my dream of owning an apartment, studying the piano, and living in the beautiful city of Paris. Now, once again, it was time to move on to the next phase of my life.

Bobby Short would often call me in California after he'd finished performing and we would chat, laugh, and discuss our personal lives. Without fail, whenever I called him, he always returned my calls within a short period. One day, the answering service (yes, he still had an answering service) picked up and, somehow, I felt an evasiveness in the operator's voice. Two days went by before I called again and got the same feeling. Then, Christina (his right-hand gal and secretary) called to let me know that Bobby had died. I hung up the phone sobbing. She later told me he'd gone into the hospital thinking his diverticulitis had become infected again. He was told he had leukemia and opted not to take the chemo or radiation but to just be kept comfortable. He died the following day.

Bobby had once confided in me he'd become bored singing the same songs night after night, and that when he looked around the cabaret room at the audience, some in love, many singing along to every song, he was somewhere else entirely, thinking about having to take out the dog when he got home, or wondering if Christina had picked up his laundry, but he was happy making so many others happy, so he kept at it.

A few weeks later, the management of the Carlyle Hotel gave a memorial cocktail party and dinner for him. During the party, filled with his closest friends, I was standing with a small group that included Chita Rivera. Looking around the room, she said, "You see these people? We will probably never see them again." Sadly, she was right. Without Bobby as our Ringmaster, none of us would have known one another.

By this time, my mentor and friend Jimmy Galanos had retired. He was commuting from Los Angeles to his Palm Springs house and began to have a series of auto accidents. None of them were serious enough to put him in a hospital, but they severely limited his ability to drive. Shortly thereafter his memory began to diminish, and the doctor concluded that Jimmy was displaying early signs of Alzheimer's Disease. His private affairs were taken over by his accountant and his wife, who installed a live-in nurse to attend to his illness.

The last time Matthew and I were with him was dinner at his favorite Sunset Towers hotel restaurant. We were four at the table and Jimmy, sitting next to me, would ask me every few minutes if I was still living in Paris. Patiently, I would reply "No" and he would continue to eat and then ask again. Seeing how bad his condition had gotten, the evening was very painful emotionally, and I realized it would likely be our last encounter.

A month after Jimmy's death, his closest friend Paul Bruggeman, and his life partner, Omar Haddadou, gave a luncheon at his Palm Springs restaurant Le Vallauris, inviting thirty of Jimmy's close friends. Among the guests were those who'd worked with him during his long career and his friends. The luncheon table was covered in one of Jimmy's favorite print fabrics: bright red poppies. Heartfelt and hilarious speeches were made, and many tears were shed. We had lost a great talent. And I had lost the kind and generous friend who helped me launch my design career.

The loss of two of my closest friends in a relatively short time left a deep void in my life. If there was a silver lining to all that loss, it was that I had come to appreciate my partner, Matthew, even more.

Love Of My Life

Architecture had always been an interest of mine, and if I hadn't gone into the fashion business, it would probably have been my career path. The midcentury modern revival explosion in the Palm Springs area piqued Matthew's and my interest, so we bought a 1957 Donald Wexler-designed house in Rancho Mirage that was being sold by the heirs of the original owner—and, like my old Paris flat, badly in need of restoration.

On Google, I discovered Wexler had gone to the University of Minnesota and was living in Palm Springs. With my usual chutzpah, I wrote to ask if he'd be interested in consulting on the restoration of the house we'd purchased. He called me saying he was retired but invited us to lunch in the desert to introduce us to an architect he recommended.

At lunch, we met the architect Lance O'Donnell, with whom we gelled immediately and felt we were in good hands. It was also during that lunch when we discovered that Wexler, who was six years older than me, had attended the same grade school, junior high, and high school as I had in North Minneapolis. An amazing coincidence.

After lunch, the four of us drove to the Rancho Mirage house. Upon entering, Wexler, who hadn't been back since it was built but remembered every detail, pointed to a wall and said it had not been there in 1957. We hired O'Donnell to commence designing the restoration immediately, and Wexler consulted as needed on the project, occasionally tweaking the plans to ensure they adhered to the original specs.

After an extensive restoration, photographs of the house appeared in *Palm Springs Life* and it was formally designated as a historical architectural landmark. The experience of owning a landmark property enabled us to become involved in the desert architectural community and participate in the founding of the Palm Springs Ed Harris Architectural Museum. However, after several years, we found the time we had to spend in the desert became more limited, and reluctantly sold the house in 2015.

In 2012, same-sex marriage was legalized across the United States, a major sea change that I never thought I'd live to see during my life. Although I'd never believed a piece of paper held two people together, I knew my love for Matthew and his love for me was permanent, and it was important to both of us to formally recognize and celebrate our love. In 2013, we decided to get married.

The Beverly Hills City Hall gave us our marriage license, but the ceremony was to be held in a tiny park in West Hollywood. Neither of us wanted anyone else to be there, but a close friend insisted on being a witness.

When the woman who officiated the wedding said the familiar words, "Do you take . . . " I began to sob. Matthew held my hands and quietly said, "Take a breath, take a deep breath." And at that, we were officially married.

As we were about to get into our car, our friend threw open his trunk and pulled out a bottle of champagne and three glasses. The three of us stood on the sidewalk toasting and drinking to our health and happiness. Matthew then went back to work, and I went home, almost as if we'd just run a quick noon-time errand. That evening, however, we hosted a small dinner at Upstairs, a favorite restaurant discreetly situated above a liquor store in West LA, so that we could celebrate our momentous day with friends.

The Benedict Canyon house I'd had for twenty-five years had always been too small for the two of us, so we agreed it was time to move. I wanted a place with lots of light and fresh air, and after some hunting around, we found and settled on a penthouse apartment that not only featured space, light, and three terraces but sat smack-dab in the middle of Beverly Hills.

The apartment had been the builder's own since being constructed in 1965 and was in the first condo building in Beverly Hills; before that, all apartments were rentals. Our apartment was in its original condition when we first saw it. I nicknamed it "Downtown Budapest," because the builder and his family had escaped the Nazis in the 1930s from Hungary, and the decor was indicative of that period with numerous chandeliers, vitrines filled with bibelots, and marble everywhere. We gutted the apartment and created an environment to fit our taste where we are happily living today.

I'm drawn to esoteric and abstract art, Latin American art, and contemporary pieces I find compelling or beguiling. The main collection is made up of contemporary work—Rauschenberg, Lichtenstein, Koons, and others. There's an Art Deco piece that I found in Antibes I've always really loved, and I remember telling Bobby Short when I first saw it that I'd have to cancel my whole summer to pay for it. I didn't buy it that year, but about a year later I saw it again in a window in Nice and bought it then, and I've never regretted it. If I see something that makes my gut tighten, no matter what period or style, if I can afford it, I buy it. Now our home is a beautiful space full of items that have captured my attention over the years.

Looking back through the decades, I have always marveled at how charmed my life has been. When I was much younger, I was embarrassed to admit where I came from. Now I relish the fact that I overcame so many hardships, and I feel a sense of pleasure telling people that I, Larry Chrysler, grew up poor in the biracial projects in Minneapolis. It's amazing how many others reveal that they, too, have come a long way, relating their own humble experiences. When we get honest about who we truly are, we forge deeper connections with those around us.

My interest in the life around me and in enjoying new experiences has not diminished, and it has been a joy being able to share all of that with the love of my life, Matthew.

2018. Matthew and I—The Happy Couple.
From the author's collection.

EPILOGUE

I was born into a cultured yet financially poor family. Deep down, I always knew there was more to this world than was presented to me. Even as a child, I couldn't relate to most of my contemporaries and often wondered if I might be adopted. Hadn't I been born a prince in some distant kingdom? Ultimately, my insatiable curiosity did indeed take me to the world's far corners, and that young boy from Minneapolis became a successful, independent adult attaining respect and recognition in the men's fashion industry.

I chose the title *Scattershot* for this memoir because it defines my life's journey as a series of often mysterious events, encounters, and adventures that enabled me to evolve from being the lone Jewish boy growing up in the Minneapolis projects to the content and comfortable man I am today. I wrote this because so many friends and business acquaintances over the years, after hearing my tales over cocktails or a meal, would exclaim, "You must write a book!" And because, at the ripe age of ninety-two, I find myself in a more reflective place than I've ever been, looking back at the many detours I've taken and wanting to make sense of it, not just for myself, but also for those who will appreciate reading about just how much life I have seen.

It's never too late to surprise yourself, explore new things—or even fall in love.

I've learned to speak multiple languages and continue to expand my horizons by being an observer of manners and maintaining an interest in all things novel and creative. I've welcomed serendipitous encounters, been unafraid to try different careers, and have always been ready to seize newfound opportunities.

I've experienced loves loved and loves lost, and watched dreams materialize before my very eyes. Yet I have never forgotten the tough times, the unhappy times, the go-hungry times that enabled that little boy in the Midwest, who dared to imagine the impossible, to live to see his lofty aspirations come true.

Many years ago, I began writing down significant memories so I would accurately remember them. As I mentioned earlier, friends often demanded I write a book recounting the many adventures in my long life. Both humorous and tragic events sometimes still unfold like a film reel in my mind's eye.

I can vividly picture the bare-chested men walking back and forth like ants in long lines unloading containers from a ship docked in Myanmar. There I was with a sarong around my waist, climbing the high concrete steps to the top of Borobudur temple in Indonesia.

I remember sweating from the high humidity as I walked among the ruins at Angkor Wat in Cambodia. Walking barefoot on the burning sandy beach at Ramatuelle near Saint Tropez. Marveling at the endless fields of lavender as I drove across the south of France. All these colorful memories and more were relived as I wrote. And yes, I remembered those sad episodes that still make me cry.

Step by step, these experiences have led to my life as it is today, and I firmly believe I have been guided by those angels the stranger saw on my shoulders so long ago. How else was it that I was often saved at the eleventh hour by unexpected opportunities thrown my way and to discover exciting new paths to follow through the years? I have never been the type of person to plan my future. I understood my inner desires but was frequently without a clue how to fulfill them, whether personal or career-wise. As I think back, I wonder why I didn't go to the Julliard School of Music in New York to inquire about a scholarship or to the Parsons School of Design. But we do what we do, and, in my case, I walked blindly through the years with the confidence that I would always be taken care of by those angels.

I have loved and been loved by wonderful people and am thankful for the two most important: Frank Tack for thirty-six years and Matthew Michael now going on twenty years. When I met Matthew, I told myself this was the man I would love till my dying day and there was no way I was going to "fuck it up" the way I might have done with Frank so many years ago. I'm pleased to report, as of this writing, I have yet to "fuck it up" with Matthew.

To many, my excitement about the notoriety and respect I attained in my retail career might seem insignificant in this world of CEOs and billionaires, but to me, who began where I did and ended up where I am, it is a wonder I frequently ponder and am grateful for.

I often reflect on how lucky I was to survive the horrors of AIDS and how much I miss those I intimately knew who died. I never did drugs, having seen up close the disastrous effects on close friends. Did I smoke a joint or two? Yes, I did, but even then, I hated the loss of control. I still drink alcohol but have never liked the effect, only the taste. "Dry Rob Roy on the rocks, please, with a lemon twist."

I never imagined or even wanted same-sex marriage to be legal, but we have come a long way, baby. I love the reactions I get when asked if Matthew and I are related and I answer, "He is my husband." It has taken years for me to say the word "husband" but now I gleefully blurt it out. What is interesting is how unconcerned people are. Yes, many have evolved, however, I still think as I did when I was bullied as a child: "Fuck 'em if they don't like it."

And on that note, I will move on to another chapter in my life and hopefully more wonderful experiences. I toast you the reader with a favorite and slightly dirty French phrase, "*Santé et bonheur, pipe à toute heure!*" Don't Google it because it ain't in the dictionary—yet.

2021. Just to see if I could still sketch.
From the author's collection.

ACKNOWLEDGMENTS

This book is a thank-you to the extraordinary individuals who have been integral to the narrative of my life, shaping the pages of this entire book with their presence and influence. I extend my heartfelt appreciation to Michael Wolfe, whose initial involvement in editing this memoir went beyond the conventional role of an editor. Michael, acting as compassionate as a therapist, skillfully delved into the depths of my emotions, unveiling sentiments about both my personal and professional journey that had long been concealed in the recesses of my soul.

My deepest thanks are reserved for my husband, Matthew Michael, whose enduring patience over our two decades together has allowed him to intimately engage with the stories I've shared. He has graciously sat through countless retellings on numerous occasions, listening with a patience that makes it seem as though each tale is being recounted for the first time.

I also want to express my sincere gratitude to Jean-Claude Magret, whose encouragement during a memorable dinner in Paris ignited the spark that led me to put pen to paper. His motivating words inspired me to capture the myriad stories that have come to define the content of this book.

ABOUT THE AUTHOR

Larry Chrysler was raised in the biracial projects of 1930s Minneapolis before pursuing a career as a dress designer in New York and Los Angeles. He eventually established himself as a distinguished menswear clothier on the iconic Rodeo Drive. Currently, Larry lives in Beverly Hills with his husband Matthew. Written in his nineties, *Scattershot: My Journey from the Projects to Paris to Rodeo Drive* is his first book.

www.ingramcontent.com/pod-product-compliance
Lightning Source LLC
Chambersburg PA
CBHW021219130626
46554CB00004B/1280